The Secret

the MAGIC™

Rhonda Byrne

ATRIA BOOKS

NEW YORK   LONDON   TORONTO   SYDNEY   NEW DELHI

Dedicated to you

May The Magic open up a new world for you,
and bring you joy for your entire existence.

That is my intention for you,
and for the world.

ACKNOWLEDGMENTS

When I first sit down to write a book, the creation begins as a joyful yet solitary one; there is just the Universe and me. Then, gradually, the circle begins to widen, encompassing more and more people, all of whom contribute their expertise, until finally you are holding the creation of a new book in your hands. The following people were a part of the ever-widening circle of creation that allowed *The Magic* to reach you.

Thank you, thank you, thank you: to my daughter Skye, who worked tirelessly side by side with me editing, along with Josh Gold, who contributed his scientific knowledge and research skills to help me unite the discoveries of science with the words of religion. Thanks to my editor, Cindy Black from Beyond Words, for her straightforward editing approach and probing questions, which have made me a better writer. Thanks to Nic George for his creative vision, which captured the magic through the interior graphics and the front cover.

To Shamus Hoare and Carla Thornton at Gozer Media, thanks for the final production of the graphics and the layout of the book. Thanks to The Secret team who help me take a new book into the world, and who are the backbone of my work; in particular my sister Jan Child, who heads up the entire publishing team; Andrea Keir, who heads up our colossal creative team; Paul Harrington and my sister Glenda Bell, who teamed up with photographer Raphael Kilpatrick and the rest of our team to create the magical pictures in this book. And thanks to the other Secret team members, whose behind-the-scenes work is invaluable: Don Zyck, Mark O'Connor, Mike Gardiner, Lori Sharapov, Cori Johansing, Chye Lee, Peter Byrne, and my daughter Hayley.

Thank you, thank you, thank you to my publishers, Atria Books and Simon & Schuster: to Carolyn Reidy, Judith Curr, Darlene DeLillo, Twisne Fan, James Pervin, Kimberly Goldstein, and Isolde Sauer. I am blessed to have such an amazing team of people.

Thank you, thank you, thank you to Angel Martin Velayos for his spiritual guidance, love, and wisdom, to my sister Pauline Vernon and my dearest friends and family for their continued support and enthusiasm for my work. And with the deepest gratitude to those great human beings of centuries ago who discovered the truths of life, and who left their written words so that we might discover them at exactly the right time – that indefinable life-changing moment when we have the eyes to see, and the ears to hear.

Contents

DO YOU BELIEVE IN MAGIC?   1

A GREAT MYSTERY IS REVEALED   5

BRING THE MAGIC INTO YOUR LIFE   15

A MAGICAL BOOK   21

Day 1 COUNT YOUR BLESSINGS   29

Day 2 THE MAGIC ROCK   37

Day 3 MAGICAL RELATIONSHIPS   43

Day 4 MAGICAL HEALTH   51

Day 5 MAGIC MONEY   61

Day 6 WORKS LIKE MAGIC   69

Day 7 THE MAGICAL WAY OUT OF NEGATIVITY   77

Day 8 THE MAGIC INGREDIENT   87

Day 9 THE MONEY MAGNET   95

Day 10 MAGIC DUST EVERYONE   101

Day 11 A MAGIC MORNING   111

Day 12 MAGICAL PEOPLE WHO MADE A DIFFERENCE   117

Day 13 MAKE ALL YOUR WISHES COME TRUE   123

Day 14 HAVE A MAGICAL DAY 133

Day 15 MAGICALLY HEAL YOUR RELATIONSHIPS 141

Day 16 MAGIC AND MIRACLES IN HEALTH 149

Day 17 THE MAGIC CHECK 157

Day 18 THE MAGICAL TO-DO LIST 167

Day 19 MAGIC FOOTSTEPS 175

Day 20 HEART MAGIC 181

Day 21 MAGNIFICENT OUTCOMES 187

Day 22 BEFORE YOUR VERY EYES 195

Day 23 THE MAGICAL AIR THAT YOU BREATHE 201

Day 24 THE MAGIC WAND 207

Day 25 CUE THE MAGIC 215

Day 26 MAGICALLY TRANSFORM MISTAKES
INTO BLESSINGS 221

Day 27 THE MAGIC MIRROR 229

Day 28 REMEMBER THE MAGIC 235

YOUR MAGICAL FUTURE 241

THE MAGIC NEVER ENDS 249

Do You Believe in Magic?

Remember when you were a child and you looked at life in total wonder and awe? Life was magical and exciting, and the smallest things were utterly thrilling to you. You were fascinated by the frost on the grass, a butterfly flittering through the air, or any strange leaf or rock on the ground.

You were full of excitement when you lost a tooth, because it meant the Tooth Fairy would be coming that night, and you would count down the days to that magical night of Christmas! Even though you had no idea how Santa Claus could get to every child in the world in one night, somehow he did it, and he never let you down.

Reindeer could fly, there were fairies in the garden, pets were like people, toys had personalities, dreams came true, and you could touch the stars. Your heart was full of joy, your imagination knew no limits, and you believed that life was magical!

There is an exquisite feeling many of us had as children, that everything is good, that every day promises more excitement and adventure, and that nothing could ever thwart our joy for the magic of it all. But somehow as we grew into adults, responsibilities, problems, and difficulties took their toll on us, we became disillusioned, and the magic we once believed in as children faded and disappeared. It's one of the reasons why as adults we love to be around children, so that we can experience that feeling we once had, even if it's just for a moment.

I am here to tell you that the magic you once believed in is true, and it's the disillusioned adult perspective of life that is false. The magic of life is *real* – and it's as real as you are. In fact, life can be far more wondrous than you ever thought it was as a child, and more breathtaking, awe-inspiring, and exciting than anything you've seen before. When you know what to do to bring forth the magic, you will live the life of your dreams. Then, you will wonder how you ever could have given up in believing in the magic of life!

You may not see reindeer fly, but you *will* see the things you've always wanted appearing before your eyes, and you will see the things you've dreamed of for so long suddenly happening. You will never know exactly how everything weaved together for your dreams to come true, because magic works in the invisible realm – and that's the most thrilling part!

Are you ready to experience the magic again? Are you ready to be filled with awe and wonder every day like when you were a child? Get ready for the magic!

Our adventure begins two thousand years ago, when life-changing knowledge was hidden within a sacred text . . .

A Great Mystery
Is Revealed

The following passage comes from the Gospel of Matthew in the Holy Scriptures, and it has mystified, confused, and been misunderstood by many people over the centuries.

"Whoever has will be given more, and he will have an abundance. Whoever does not have, even what he has will be taken from him."

You have to admit that when you read the passage it appears unjust, as it seems to be saying that the rich will get richer and the poor will get poorer. But there's a riddle to be solved in this passage, a mystery to uncover, and when you know it a new world will have opened up for you.

The answer to the mystery that has eluded so many for centuries is in one hidden word: **gratitude**.

*"Whoever has **gratitude** will be given more, and he or she will have an abundance. Whoever does not have **gratitude**, even what he or she has will be taken from him or her."*

By the revelation of one hidden word, a cryptic text is made crystal clear. Two thousand years have passed since those words were recorded, but they are as true today as they ever were: if you don't take the time to be grateful you will never have more, and what you do have you will lose. And the promise of the magic that will happen with gratitude is in these words: *if you're grateful you will be given more, and you will have an abundance!*

From the Koran the promise of gratitude is equally emphatic:

"And (remember) when God proclaimed: 'If you are grateful I will give you more; but if you are ungrateful verily my punishment is indeed severe.'"

It doesn't matter what religion you follow, or whether you're religious or not, these words from the Holy Scriptures and the Koran apply to you and your life. They are describing a fundamental law of science and of the Universe.

It's Universal Law

Gratitude operates through a Universal law that governs your whole life. According to the law of attraction, which governs all the energy in our Universe, from the formation of an atom to the movement of the planets, "like attracts like." It's because of the law of attraction that the cells of every living creature are held together, as well as the substance of every material object. In your life, the law operates on your thoughts and feelings, because they are energy too, and so whatever you think, whatever you feel, you attract to you.

If you think, "I don't like my job," "I haven't got enough money," "I can't find my perfect partner," "I can't pay my bills," "I think I'm coming down with something," "He or she doesn't appreciate me," "I don't get along with my parents," "My child is a problem," "My life is a mess," or "My marriage is in trouble," then you must attract more of those experiences.

But if you think about what you're grateful for, like, "I love my job," "My family is very supportive," "I had the best vacation," "I feel amazing today," "I got the biggest tax refund ever," or "I had a great weekend camping with my son," and you sincerely feel the gratitude, the law of attraction says you must attract more of *those* things into your life. It works in the same way as metal being drawn to a magnet; your gratitude is magnetic, and the more gratitude you have, the more abundance you magnetize. It is Universal law!

You will have heard sayings like, "Whatever goes around comes around," "You reap what you sow," and "You get what you give." Well, all of those sayings are describing the same law, and they're also describing a principle of the Universe that the great scientist Sir Isaac Newton discovered.

Newton's scientific discoveries included the fundamental laws of motion in the Universe, one of which says:

Every action always has an opposite and equal reaction.

When you apply the idea of gratitude to Newton's law it says: every action of *giving* thanks always causes an opposite reaction of *receiving*. And what you receive will always be equal to the amount of gratitude you've given. This means that the very action of gratitude sets off a reaction of receiving! And the more sincerely and the more deeply grateful you feel (in other words, the *more* gratitude you give) the *more* you will receive.

The Golden Thread of Gratitude

Dating back thousands and thousands of years to the earliest recordings of humankind, the power of gratitude was preached and practiced, and from there was passed on through the centuries, sweeping across the continents, permeating one civilization and culture to the next. The major religions of Christianity, Islam, Judaism, Buddhism, Sikhism, and Hinduism all have gratitude at their core.

Muhammad said that gratitude for the abundance you've received is the best insurance that the abundance will continue.

Buddha said that you have no cause for anything but gratitude and joy.

Lao Tzu said that if you rejoice in the way things are, the whole world will belong to you.

Krishna said that whatever he is offered he accepts with joy.

King David spoke of giving thanks to the whole world, for everything between the heavens and the Earth.

And Jesus said *thank you* before he performed each miracle.

From the Australian Aborigines to the African Maasai and Zulu, from the American Navajo, Shawnee, and Cherokee, to the Tahitians, Eskimo, and Maori, the practice of gratitude is at the very root of most indigenous traditions.

> *"When you arise in the morning, give thanks for the morning light, for your life and strength. Give thanks for your food and the joy of living. If you see no reason for giving thanks, the fault lies with yourself."*
>
> TECUMSEH (1768–1813)
> SHAWNEE NATIVE AMERICAN LEADER

History is laden with famous figures who practiced gratitude, and whose achievements put them amongst the greatest human beings who have ever lived: Gandhi, Mother Teresa, Martin Luther King Jr., the Dalai Lama, Leonardo Da Vinci, Plato, Shakespeare, Aesop, Blake, Emerson, Dickens, Proust, Descartes, Lincoln, Jung, Newton, Einstein, and many, many more.

Albert Einstein's scientific discoveries changed the way we see the Universe, and when asked about his monumental achievements, he spoke only of giving thanks to others. One of the most brilliant minds of all time thanked other people over a hundred times a day for the work they had done!

Is it any wonder that so many of life's mysteries were revealed to Albert Einstein? Is it any wonder that Albert Einstein made some of the greatest scientific discoveries in history? He practiced gratitude every single day of his life, and in return he received many forms of abundance.

When Isaac Newton was asked how he had achieved the scientific discoveries he made, he said that he stood on the shoulders of giants. Isaac Newton, recently voted the greatest contributor to science and humankind, was also *grateful* to those men and women who lived before him.

The scientists, philosophers, inventors, discoverers, and prophets who practiced gratitude reaped its results, and most were aware of its inherent power. Yet still gratitude's power is unknown to most people today, because to experience the magic of gratitude in your life you have to practice it!

My Discovery

My story is a perfect example of what life is like when a person is ignorant of gratitude, and what happens when you make gratitude a part of your life.

If I had been asked six years ago if I was a grateful person, I would have answered, "Yes, for sure I'm a grateful person. I say thank you when I receive a gift, when someone opens a door for me, or when a person does something for me."

The truth is I was not a grateful person at all. I didn't know what being grateful *really* meant, and just saying the words *thank you* on the odd occasion certainly didn't make me a grateful person.

My life without gratitude was pretty challenging. I was in debt, and it was increasing a little bit more every month. I worked really hard, but my finances never improved. In trying to keep up with the mounting debt and obligations I was living with a continuous undercurrent of stress. My relationships swung like a pendulum from fair to disastrous, because I never seemed to have enough time for each person.

While I was what would be termed "healthy," I felt exhausted at the end of each day, and I always got my fair share of colds and the latest illnesses going around each season. I had moments of happiness when I went out with friends, or when I went on vacation, but then the reality of having to work harder to pay for those pleasures would sweep over me.

I wasn't living. I was surviving – from day to day and from paycheck to paycheck, and I would no sooner solve one life problem than more problems would appear.

But then something happened that would change everything in my life from that day forward. I discovered a secret about life, and as a result of my discovery one of the things I began to do was practice gratitude each day. As a result of this, everything in my life changed, and the more I practiced gratitude, the more miraculous were the results. My life truly became magical.

For the first time in my life I became debt free, and shortly after that I had all the money I needed to do whatever I wanted. Problems in my relationships, work, and health disappeared, and instead of facing daily obstacles, my days became filled with one good thing after another. My health and energy increased dramatically, and I felt better than I had in my twenties. My relationships became much more meaningful, and I enjoyed more good times with my family and friends in just a few months than I had in all the previous years.

More than anything else, I felt happier than I thought it was possible to feel. I was blissfully happy – the happiest I had ever been. Gratitude changed me, and my whole life magically changed.

Bring The Magic into Your Life

No matter who you are, no matter where you are, no matter what your current circumstances, the magic of gratitude will change your entire life!

I have received letters from thousands of people in the worst imaginable situations who have changed their lives completely by practicing gratitude. I have seen miracles take place in health where there seemed to be no hope. I have seen marriages saved, and broken relationships transform into magnificent relationships. I have seen those in total poverty become prosperous, and I have seen people in depression catapult into joyful and fulfilling lives.

Gratitude can magically turn your relationships into joyful and meaningful relationships, no matter what state they are in now. Gratitude can miraculously make you more prosperous so that you have the money you need to do the things you want to do. It will increase your health and bring a level of happiness beyond what you've ever felt before. Gratitude will work its magic to accelerate your career, increase success, and bring about your dream job or whatever it is you want to do. In fact, whatever it is that you want to be, do, or have, gratitude is the way to receive it. The magical power of gratitude turns your life into gold!

As you practice gratitude, you will understand why particular things in your life may have gone wrong, and why certain things might be missing from your life. As you make gratitude a way of life, you will wake up each morning so excited to be alive. You will find yourself completely in love with life. Everything will seem effortless. You will feel as light as a feather and happier than you've ever felt before. While challenges may come, you will know how to overcome them and learn from them. Every day will be magical; every day will be filled with far more magic than when you were a child.

Is Your Life Magical?

You can tell right now how much you have actually used gratitude in your life. Just take a look at all of the major areas in your life: money, health, happiness, career, home, and relationships. The areas of your life that are abundant and wonderful are where you have used gratitude and are experiencing the magic as a result. Any areas that are not abundant and wonderful are due to a lack of gratitude.

It's a simple fact: when you're not grateful you cannot receive more in return. You've stopped the magic from continuing in your life. When you're not grateful you stop the flow of better health, better relationships, more joy, more money, and the advancement of your job, career, or business. To *receive* you have to *give*. It's the law. Gratitude is *giving* thanks, and without it you cut yourself off from the magic and from *receiving* everything you want in life.

The bottom line of ungratefulness is that when we're not grateful, we're *taking*; we're taking things in our life for granted. When we take things for granted we are unintentionally taking from ourselves. The law of attraction says that like attracts like, so if we take something for granted, we will be taken from as a result. Remember, "whoever does not have **gratitude**, even what he or she has will be taken from him or her."

Most certainly you have been grateful at various times in your life, but to see the magic and cause a radical change to your current circumstances, you have to practice gratitude and make it your new way of life.

The Magic Formula

"Knowledge is a treasure, but practice is the key to it."
IBN KHALDOUN AL MUQADDIMA (1332–1406)
SCHOLAR AND STATESMAN

Ancient myths and legends say that to bring forth magic a person must first say "the magic words." Bringing forth magic from gratitude works in the same way, and first you must say the magic words: *thank you.* I cannot begin to tell you how important the words *thank you* are for your life. To live in gratitude, to experience the magic in your life, *thank you* must become the two words you deliberately say and feel more than any other words. They need to become your identity. *Thank you* is the bridge from where you are now, to the life of your dreams.

The Magic Formula:

1. Deliberately think and say the magic words, *thank you.*

2. The more you deliberately think and say the magic words, *thank you,* the more gratitude you feel.

3. The more gratitude you deliberately think and feel, the more abundance you receive.

Gratitude is a feeling. So the ultimate aim in practicing gratitude is to deliberately *feel* it as much as you can, because it's the force of your feeling that accelerates the magic in your life. Newton's law is one for one – what you give you receive, equally. That means that if you increase your feeling of gratitude, the results in your life will expand to be *equal* to your feeling! The truer the feeling, the more sincerely grateful you are, the faster your life will change.

When you discover how little practice it takes, how easy it is to incorporate gratitude into your daily life, and when you see the magical results for yourself, you will never want to return to the life you used to live.

If you practice gratitude a little, your life will change a little. If you practice gratitude a lot every day, your life will change dramatically and in ways that you can hardly imagine.

A Magical Book

"As we express our gratitude, we must never forget that the highest appreciation is not to utter words, but to live by them."

JOHN F. KENNEDY (1917–1963)
35TH PRESIDENT OF THE UNITED STATES

In this book, there are 28 magical practices that have been specifically designed so that you learn how to use gratitude's magical power to revolutionize your health, money, job, and relationships, and to make your smallest desires and your biggest dreams come true. You will also learn how to practice gratitude to dissolve problems and transform any negative situation.

You will be captivated while you read this life-changing knowledge, but without practicing what you learn, the knowledge will slip through your fingers, and the opportunity that you attracted to easily change your life will be gone. To ensure this doesn't happen to you, you need to practice gratitude over 28 days, so that you impregnate your cells and your subconscious mind with it. Only then will it change your life – permanently.

The practices are designed to be completed over 28 consecutive days. This allows you to make gratitude a habit and a new way of life. Practicing gratitude in a concentrated effort over consecutive days guarantees that you will see the magic take place in your life – and fast!

Within each magical practice is a wealth of secret teachings that will expand your knowledge in tremendous ways. In each practice you will understand more and more about how life works, and how easy it is to have the life you've dreamed of.

The first twelve practices use the magical power of gratitude for what you have now and for what you've received in the past, because unless you're grateful for what you have, and what you've received, the magic won't work and you won't receive more. These first twelve practices will set the magic of gratitude into motion immediately.

The next ten practices use the magical power of gratitude for your desires, dreams, and everything you want. Through these ten practices you will be able to make your dreams come true, and you will see the circumstances of your life magically change!

The last six practices take you to a whole new level, where you will be saturating gratitude into every cell of your body and mind. You will learn how to use gratitude's magical power to help other people, dissolve problems, and improve any negative situation or circumstance you may encounter throughout your life.

You don't need to clear your calendar, because each of the practices has been specifically created to fit into your everyday life, whether it's workdays, weekends, holidays, or vacations. Gratitude is portable – you take it with you wherever *you* go, and then wherever *you* go, the magic happens!

If you miss a day, you will most likely lose the momentum of what you have done. To ensure that you don't reduce the magic, if you miss a day, count back three days and repeat the practices again from there.

Some practices are designed for the morning, and others are designed to do throughout the day, so read each day's practice first thing in the morning. Some practices will need to be read the night before because they begin when you wake, and I will tell you when to do this. You might want to read the next day's practice every night before you go to sleep, in order to be prepared. If you do, make sure to reread the practice again in the morning.

If you don't want to follow the 28 magical practices consecutively, you can also use them in other ways. You could choose one magical practice that addresses an important subject in your life that you want to change or improve, and you could do that practice three days in a row or every day for a week. Or you could do one magical practice a week, or two practices a week, the only difference being that it will take you longer to see the changes in your life.

After the 28 Days

Once you've completed the 28 magical practices, you can use particular practices to increase the magic where or when you have a specific need, such as for health or money, or if you want to receive your dream job, have increased success in your work, or improve a relationship. Or to continue the practice of gratitude you can open this book at random, and whichever practice you open to is the one you attracted, so it's the perfect one to do that day.

At the end of the 28 magical practices, there are also recommendations of practices you can use in combination, which will accelerate the magic in specific areas of your life.

Can you overdo gratitude? Never! Can your life become too magical? Hardly! Use the practices over and over, so that gratitude seeps into your consciousness and becomes second nature to you. After 28 days you will have rewired your brain, and implanted gratitude in your subconscious mind, where it is automatically the first thing that comes to your mind in any situation. The magic you experience will be your inspiration, because as you incorporate gratitude into your days, they will be nothing short of spectacular!

What Are Your Dreams?

Many of the magical practices are designed to help you achieve your dreams. Therefore, you need to get clear about what you *really* want.

Sit down with a computer or pen and paper and make a list of what you really want in every area of your life. Think through every detail of what you want to be, do, or have in your life – in your relationships, career, finances, health, and every area that is important to you. You can be as specific and detailed as you like, but remember your job is simply to list what you want, not how you're going to get what you want. The "how" will be done *for* you when gratitude works its magic.

If you want a better job, or your dream job, then think about everything you want the job to be. Think about the things that are important to you, such as the type of work you want to do, how you want to feel in your job, the type of company you want to work for, the kind of people you want to work with, the hours you want to work, where you want your job to be, and the salary you want to receive. Get very clear about what you want in the job by thinking it through thoroughly and writing all the details down.

If you want money to educate your children, work out the details of their education, including which school you want your children to attend, the cost of the school fees, books, food, clothing, and transportation, so that you know exactly how much money you will need.

If you want to travel, then write down the details of the countries you want to visit, how long you want to travel for, what you want to see and do, where you want to stay, and the means by which you want to travel.

If you want a perfect partner, then write down every detail of the characteristics you want that person to have. If you want improved relationships, write down the relationships you want to improve, and what you want them to be like.

If you want more health, or an improved bodily condition, be specific about what ways you want to improve your health or body. If you want a dream home, then list every detail of what you want the home to be, room by room. If there are specific material things you want, like a car, clothes, or appliances, write them down.

If you want to achieve something, such as passing an exam, getting a degree, a goal in sports, succeeding as a musician, doctor, writer, actor, scientist, or businessperson, or whatever it is you would like to achieve, write it down and be as specific as possible.

I would strongly urge you to find the time to maintain a list of your dreams throughout your life. Write down the little things, the big things, or what you want this moment, this month, or this year. As you think of more things add them to the list, and as you receive things, cross them off the list. An easy way to do a list of what you want is to divide it into categories of:

Health and body

Career and work

Money

Relationships

Personal desires

Material things

And then just add the things you want to each category.

When you get clear about the things you want, you are giving a definite direction to the way you want gratitude's magical power to change your life, and you are ready to begin the most exciting and thrilling adventure you've ever been on!

Day 1
COUNT YOUR BLESSINGS

*"When I started counting my blessings, my whole life
turned around."*

WILLIE NELSON (B. 1933)
SINGER-SONGWRITER

You will have heard people say to count your
blessings, and when you think about the things you're
grateful for, that's exactly what you're doing. But
what you may not have realized is that counting your
blessings is one of the most powerful practices you
can ever do, and it will magically turn your whole
life around!

When you're grateful for the things you have, no
matter how small they may be, you will see those things
instantly increase. If you're grateful for the money you
have, however little, you will see your money magically
grow. If you're grateful for a relationship, even if it's not
perfect, you will see it miraculously get even better. If
you're grateful for the job that you have, even if it's not

29

your dream job, things will begin to change so that you enjoy your job more, and all kinds of opportunities for your work will suddenly appear.

The flipside is that when we're not counting our blessings, we can fall into the trap of unintentionally counting negative things. We count negative things when we talk about the things we don't have. We count negative things when we criticize or find fault with other people, when we complain about traffic, waiting in lines, delays, the government, not enough money, or the weather. When we count negative things they increase too, but on top of that, with every negative thing we count, we cancel out blessings that were on their way. I have tried both – counting my blessings and counting negative things – and I can assure you that counting your blessings is the only way to have abundance in your life.

> *"Better to lose count while naming your blessings than to lose your blessings to counting your troubles."*
>
> MALTBIE D. BABCOCK (1858–1901)
> WRITER AND CLERGYMAN

First thing in the morning, or as early in the day as you can, Count Your Blessings. You can write out your list by hand, type it on a computer, or use a special book or journal and keep all of your gratitude in one place. Today, you are going to make a simple list of ten blessings in your life you are grateful for.

When Einstein gave thanks, he thought about *why* he was grateful. When you think about the reason *why* you're grateful for a particular thing, person, or situation, you will feel gratitude more deeply. Remember that the magic of gratitude happens according to the degree of your feeling! So with each item on your list write the reason why you're grateful for it.

Here are some ideas for writing your list:

- *I am truly blessed to have ____ what? ____, because ____ why? ____.*

- *I am so happy and grateful for ____ what? ____, because ____ why? ____.*

- *I am truly grateful for ____ what? ____, because ____ why? ____.*

- *With all my heart, thank you for ____ what? ____, because ____ why? ____.*

After you've finished making your list of ten blessings, go back and read each one, either in your mind or out loud. When you get to the end of each blessing, say the magic words three times, *thank you, thank you, thank you,* and feel the gratitude for that blessing as much as you possibly can.

To help you feel more gratitude, you can be grateful to the Universe, God, Spirit, goodness, life, your greater self, or any other concept you are drawn to. When you direct gratitude toward something or someone, you will feel it even more, and your gratitude will have even more power, and create even more magic! It's the reason why indigenous and ancient cultures chose symbols like the sun to direct their gratitude toward. They were simply using physical symbols to represent the universal source of all goodness, and in focusing on that symbol they felt more gratitude.

The practice of counting your blessings is so simple and so powerful in altering your life, that I want you to continue to add ten more blessings to your list every day for the next 27 days. You might think it could be difficult to find ten things you're grateful for every day, but the more you think about it, the more you will realize *how much you have to be grateful for.* Look closely at your life; you have received, and are continuing to receive so much each and every day. There is really *so* much to give thanks for!

You could be grateful for your home, your family, your friends, your work, and your pets. You could be thankful for the sun, the water that you drink, the food that you eat, and the air that you breathe; without any of them you wouldn't be alive. You could be grateful for the trees, the animals, the oceans, the birds, the flowers, the plants, blue skies, rain, the stars, the moon, and our beautiful planet Earth.

You could be grateful for your senses: your eyes that see, your ears that hear, your mouth that tastes, your nose that smells, and your skin that enables you to feel. You could be grateful for the legs you walk on, your hands that you use to do almost everything, your voice that enables you to express yourself and communicate with others. You could give thanks for your amazing immune system that keeps you well, and all of your organs that maintain your body so that you can live. And what about the magnificence of your human mind, which no computer technology in the world can duplicate?

Here is a list of subjects that will remind you of the major areas you can look for blessings to be grateful for. You can also add any subject you want depending on what is important to you at any time.

Magic Gratitude Subjects:

- *Health and body*

- *Work and success*

- *Money*

- *Relationships*

- *Passions*

- *Happiness*

- *Love*

- *Life*

- *Nature: planet Earth, air, water, and the sun*

- *Material goods and services*

- *Any subject of your choosing*

You should feel significantly better and happier after each time you Count Your Blessings, and how good you feel is your measure of how much gratitude you felt. The more gratitude you felt, the happier you will feel, and the faster your life will change. Some days you will feel happy really quickly, and other days it may take a little longer. But as you continue to Count Your Blessings every day, you will notice a bigger and bigger difference in the way you feel each time, and you will see your blessings magically multiply!

Magic Reminder

Make sure to read tomorrow's magical practice sometime today, as you will need to do something specific before you begin tomorrow.

MAGIC PRACTICE NUMBER 1

Count Your Blessings

1. First thing in the morning, make a list of **ten** blessings in your life you are grateful for.

2. Write *why* you're grateful for each blessing.

3. Go back and read your list, either in your mind or out loud. When you get to the end of each one, say the magic words, *thank you, thank you, thank you,* and feel the gratitude for that blessing as much as you possibly can.

4. Repeat the first three steps of this magical practice every morning for the next 27 days.

5. Read tomorrow's magical practice today.

Day 2
THE MAGIC ROCK

"Reflect upon your present blessings of which every man has plenty; not on your past misfortunes of which all men have some."

CHARLES DICKENS (1812–1870)
WRITER

In the beginning of working with these practices, it takes concentrated days in a row to make gratitude a habit. Anything that reminds you to be grateful is helping you turn your life into gold with gratitude, and that's exactly what this magical practice is about.

Lee Brower presented the gratitude rock practice in *The Secret* film and book, when he told us the story of the father of a dying child who used a gratitude rock to be grateful for his son's health, and his son made a miraculous recovery. Since then the gratitude rock has been a proven success with many people the world over, who have used it for money, healing, and happiness.

First, find a rock or a stone. Choose a small size that fits in the palm of your hand and that you can close your fingers around. Choose a rock that is smooth, without sharp edges, not too weighty, and that feels really good in your hand when you hold it.

You can find a Magic Rock from your garden if you have one, or from a riverbed, creek, ocean, or park. If you don't have easy access to any of these places, then ask your neighbors, family, or friends. You may even have a precious rock or stone already that you can use as your Magic Rock.

When you have found your Magic Rock, put it by your bedside, in a place where you will definitely see it when you go to bed. Clear some space if necessary so that you can easily see your Magic Rock when you go to bed. If you use an alarm clock, put it next to your alarm clock.

Tonight, just before you get into bed to go to sleep, pick up your Magic Rock, hold it in the palm of one hand, and close your fingers around it.

Think back carefully through all the good things that happened during the day, and find *the best thing* that happened that you're grateful for. Then say the magic words, *thank you,* for the best thing that happened. Return the Magic Rock to its place by your bed. And that's it!

Every night for the next 26 days, follow the same Magic Rock practice. Before you go to sleep, think back through the day, and find the *best* thing that happened that day. While holding your Magic Rock in your hand, be as grateful as you can be for that thing, and say *thank you.*

Using a rock seems like such a simple thing to do, but through this practice you will see magical things begin to happen in your life.

When you look for the *best* thing that happened during the day, you will search through many good things that happened, and in the process of searching and then deciding on the *best* one you are actually thinking of many things you're grateful for. You will also be ensuring that you go to sleep and wake up in gratitude each day.

The Count Your Blessings and Magic Rock practices will ensure that you begin and end your days in a state of gratitude. In fact, they are so powerful that together they would change your life in a few months. But this book is designed to change your life really fast through an abundance of magical practices. Because gratitude is magnetic and attracts more things to be grateful for, the concentration of gratitude over 28 days will intensify the magnetic force of your gratitude. When you have a strong magnetic force of gratitude, like magic, you automatically magnetize everything you want and need to you!

Magic Reminder

Be sure to read tomorrow's magical practice sometime today, as you will need to collect some photographs before you begin.

MAGIC PRACTICE NUMBER 2

The Magic Rock

1. Repeat steps one to three of Magic Practice Number 1 – Count Your Blessings: Make a list of ten blessings. Write *why* you're grateful. Reread your list, and at the end of each blessing say *thank you, thank you, thank you,* and feel as grateful for that blessing as you can.

2. Find a Magic Rock and put it by your bedside.

3. Before going to sleep tonight, hold your Magic Rock in your hand and think of *the best thing* that happened today.

4. Say the magic words, *thank you,* for the best thing that happened today.

5. Repeat the Magic Rock practice every night for the next 26 days.

6. Read tomorrow's magical practice today.

Day 3
MAGICAL RELATIONSHIPS

Imagine if you were the only person on Earth; you would have no desire to do anything. What would be the point in creating a painting if no one could see it? What would be the point in composing music if no one could hear it? What would be the point in inventing anything if there was no one to use it? There would be no reason to move from one place to another because wherever you went would be the same as where you were – no one would be there. There would be no pleasure or joy in your life.

It's your contact and experiences with other people that give your life joy, meaning, and purpose. Because of that, your relationships affect your life more than anything else. To receive the life of your dreams, it's vital that you understand how your relationships affect your life now, and how they are the most powerful channels for gratitude to start magically changing your life.

Science is now confirming the wisdom of the great sages of the past, with research studies showing that people who practice gratitude have closer relationships, are more connected to family and friends, and have other people look upon them favorably. But probably the most astounding statistic that has come out of research studies is that for every *one* complaint about another person, whether in thought or word, there have to be *ten* blessings for the relationship to flourish. Any less than ten blessings for every one complaint and the relationship will deteriorate, and, if the relationship is a marriage, it will most likely end in divorce.

Gratitude makes relationships flourish. As you increase your gratitude for any relationship, you will magically receive an abundance of happiness and good things in that relationship. And gratitude for your relationships doesn't change only your relationships; it also changes you. No matter what your temperament is now, gratitude will give you more patience, understanding, compassion, and kindness, to the point where you won't even recognize yourself. The little irritations you once felt and the complaints you had in your relationships will disappear, because when you're truly grateful for another person, there's nothing you want to change about that person. You won't criticize, complain about, or blame them, because you're too busy being grateful for the good things about them. In fact, you won't even be able to see the things you used to complain about.

*"We can only be said to be alive in those moments when
our hearts are conscious of our treasures."*

THORNTON WILDER (1897–1975)
WRITER AND PLAYWRIGHT

Words are very powerful, so when you complain about
any person you actually harm *your* life. It is *your* life that
will suffer. By the law of attraction whatever you think
or say about another person, you bring to you. This is
the very reason why the greatest minds and teachers
of the world have told us to be grateful. They knew
that for you to receive more in *your* life, for *your* life to
magically increase, you have to be grateful for others
just as they are. What if every person close to you said,
"I love you – just the way you are," how would you feel?

Today's magical practice is being grateful for people
just as they are! Even if all of your relationships
are currently good, they will increase with more
magnificence through this practice. And with
everything you find to be grateful for in each person,
you will see gratitude perform its breathtaking magic,
and your relationships will be stronger, more fulfilling,
and more enriching than you ever thought they
could be.

Choose three of your closest relationships to be grateful
for. You might choose your wife, your son, and your
father, or your boyfriend, your business partner, and
your sister. You might choose your best friend, your
grandmother, and your uncle. You can choose any three
relationships that are important to you, as long as you

have a photograph of each person. The photograph can be just of the person, or the both of you together.

Once you have selected your three relationships and photographs, you are ready to set the magic into motion. Sit down and think about the things you are the most grateful for about each person. What are the things you love the most about this person? What are their best qualities? You could be grateful for their patience, ability to listen, talents, strength, good judgment, wisdom, laugh, sense of humor, eyes, smile, or kind heart. You could be grateful for the things you enjoy doing with the person, or you can recall a time when the person was there for you, cared for, or supported you.

After you've spent some time thinking about what you're grateful for about the person, put their photograph in front of you, and with a pen and notebook, or on your computer, choose the five things you are the most grateful for. Look at the photograph of the person as you make your list of five things, begin each sentence with the magic words, *thank you,* address the person by their name, and then write what you're grateful for.

Thank you, _____*their name*_____, *for* ____*what?*____ .

For example, "Thank you, John, for always making me laugh." Or, "Thank you, Mom, for supporting me through college."

When you've finished your lists for all three people, continue with this magical practice by taking the photographs with you today and putting them in a place where you will see them often. Whenever you look at the photographs today, thank the person by saying the magic words, *thank you,* and the person's name:

Thank you, Hayley.

If you're moving around a lot, carry the photographs with you in your bag or pocket, and make an effort to look at the photographs three times during the day, following the same procedure.

Now you know how to use gratitude's magical power to transform your relationships into Magical Relationships. Although it is not part of the requirement of this book, you may want to take this amazing practice and use it every day if necessary to make every relationship you have magnificent. You can use it on the same relationship as many times as you want. The more you can be grateful for the good things in your relationships, the faster every relationship in your life will miraculously change.

Magic Practice Number 3

Magical Relationships

1. Repeat steps one to three of Magic Practice Number 1 – Count Your Blessings: Make a list of ten blessings. Write *why* you're grateful. Reread your list, and at the end of each blessing say *thank you, thank you, thank you,* and feel as grateful for that blessing as you can.

2. Choose **three** of your closest relationships and collect a photograph of each person.

3. With the photo in front of you, write **five** things you are most grateful for about each person, in your journal or on your computer.

4. Begin each sentence with the magic words, *thank you,* include their name, and what you're specifically grateful for.

5. Carry the three photographs with you today, or put them in a place where you will see them often. Look at the photographs on at least **three** occasions, speak to the person's face in the photograph, and thank them by saying the magic words, *thank you,* and their name. *Thank you, Hayley.*

6. Before you go to sleep, take your Magic Rock in one hand, and say the magic words, *thank you,* for the *best* thing that happened during the day.

Day 4
MAGICAL HEALTH

"The greatest wealth is health."

VIRGIL (70 BC–19 BC)
ROMAN POET

Health is the most precious thing in life, and yet more than anything else, we can take our health for granted. For many of us, the only time we think of our health is when we lose it. Then the realization hits us: without our health, we have nothing.

There's an Italian proverb that speaks the truth about health for many of us: "He who enjoys good health is rich, though he knows it not." While we rarely think of our health when we are well, you will have felt the truth of those words even when you had something minor like a cold or the flu, and you were bedridden. When you are not well, all you want is to feel better, and nothing else matters other than having your health back again.

Health is a gift of life; it is something you receive and continue to receive, each day. In addition to everything else we do to be healthy, we have to be grateful for our health to continue to receive more health!

Remember:

*"Whoever has **gratitude** (for health) will be given more, and he or she will have an abundance. Whoever does not have **gratitude** (for health), even what he or she has will be taken from him or her."*

You may know of people who chose a healthy lifestyle and yet still lost their health. *Giving* thanks in return for the health you are *receiving* is vital. When you are grateful for your health, you will not only maintain your current health, at the same time you will set the magic into motion to increase the flow of health to you. You will also begin to see the improvements to your health happen right away. Little aches and pains, moles, scars, or marks will start to magically disappear, and you will notice your energy, vitality, and happiness increase markedly.

As you will learn in a later practice, through the daily practice of gratitude for your health, you can improve your eyesight, hearing, and all of your senses, along with every function in your entire body. And all of it happens like magic!

"Gratitude is a vaccine, an antitoxin,
and an antiseptic."

JOHN HENRY JOWETT (1864–1923)
PRESBYTERIAN PREACHER AND WRITER

The degree that you are grateful for your health is the exact degree that your health will magically increase, and the degree that you're not grateful is the exact degree that your health will decrease. Living with a decreased amount of health means your energy, vitality, immune system, clarity of thought, and every other function of your body and mind is weakened.

Being grateful for your health ensures that you will continue to receive more health to be grateful for, and at the same time it eliminates stress and tension in your body and mind. Scientific research studies have shown that stress and tension are at the root of many diseases. Studies have also revealed that people who practice gratitude heal faster, and are likely to live seven years longer!

You can see in the state of your health right now how grateful you have been. You should feel amazing every day. If you feel heavy and life feels like a real effort to get through, or if you don't feel younger than your age, then you are living with decreased health. One of the major causes of this loss of vitality is a lack of gratitude. All of that is about to change, though, because you are going to use gratitude's magical power for the health of your body!

The Magical Health practice begins with reading through the following paragraphs about the health of your body. After you read each italicized line for a particular part of your body, close your eyes and mentally repeat the italicized line, feeling as grateful as you can for that part of your body. Remember that when you think about *why* you're grateful, it will help you feel gratitude more deeply, and the deeper you feel it, the faster you will feel and see the amazing results in your body.

Think about your legs and feet; they are your main form of transportation in your life. Think about all the things you use your legs for, like balancing, standing up, sitting down, exercising, dancing, climbing steps, driving a car, and, most of all, the miracle of walking. Your legs and feet allow you to walk around your home, walk to the bathroom, go to the kitchen to get a drink, and walk to your car. Your legs and feet allow you to walk around stores, down the streets, through an airport, and along the beach. The ability to walk gives us freedom to enjoy life! Say *thank you for my legs and feet,* and really mean it.

Think about your arms and hands and how many things you pick up and hold in one day. Your hands are the major tools of your life, and they are in nonstop use all day long, every day. Your hands allow you to write, eat a meal, use a phone or computer, shower, get dressed, use the bathroom, pick up things and hold them, and do everything for yourself. Without the use of your hands you would be dependent on other people to do things for you. Say *thank you for my arms, hands, and fingers!*

Think about your amazing senses. Your sense of taste gives you so much pleasure multiple times throughout the day as you eat and drink. You know from losing your sense of taste through a cold that the joy of eating and drinking disappears without being able to taste food or drinks. Say *thank you for my amazing sense of taste!*

Your sense of smell enables you to experience the beautiful fragrances of life: flowers, perfumes, clean sheets, dinner as it's cooking, a fire burning on a winter's night, the air on a summer's day, freshly cut grass, the smell of the earth after rain. Say *thank you for my wonderful sense of smell!*

If you didn't have a sense of touch, you would never know hot from cold, soft from sharp, or smooth from rough. You would never be able to feel objects, or physically express love or receive it. Your sense of touch allows you to touch your loved ones with a reassuring hug, and to feel the touch of a hand from one human being to another is one of the most precious things in life. Say *thank you for my precious sense of touch!*

Think about the miracle of your eyes, which enable you to see the faces of your loved ones and friends, read printed books, newspapers, and emails, watch television, see the beauty of nature, and, most importantly, see your way through life. Just put a blindfold on for an hour and try to do what you normally do, and you will appreciate your eyes. Say *thank you for my eyes that enable me to see everything!*

Think about your ears, which enable you to hear your own voice and other people's voices so you can talk to people. Without ears and your sense of hearing you could not use a phone, hear music, listen to the radio, hear your loved ones talk, or hear any of the sounds of the world around you. Say *thank you for my hearing!*

And to use any of your senses would be impossible without your brain, which processes over a million messages a second through all of your senses! It is actually your brain that enables you to sense and experience life, and there is no computer technology in the world that can duplicate it. Say *thank you for my brain and my beautiful mind!*

Think about the trillions of cells working unceasingly, 24/7, for your health, body, and life. Say *thank you cells!* Think about your life-sustaining organs, which are continuously filtering, cleaning, and renewing everything in your body, and think about the fact that they do all their work automatically without you even having to think about it. Say *thank you, organs, for working perfectly!*

But more miraculous than any sense, system, function, or other organ in our body, is the organ of your heart. Your heart governs the life of every other organ, because it is your heart that keeps the life flowing to every system in your body. Say *thank you for my strong and healthy heart!*

Next, take a piece of paper or a card, and write on it in big bold letters:

THE GIFT OF HEALTH IS KEEPING ME ALIVE.

Take the card with you today, and put it in a place where you know you will see it often. If you work at a desk, you can put it right in front of you. If you're a driver, put it in a place in your car or truck where you will see it often. If you're at home most of the time, you can put it where you wash your hands, or near your phone. Choose a place where you know you will see the words you've written often.

Today, on at least four separate occasions, when you see the words read them very slowly, one word at a time, and feel as grateful as you can for the gift of health.

Being grateful for your health is essential to keep your health, but also to guarantee that it continues to get better, with increasing energy and zest for life. If gratitude were used in conjunction with conventional medical treatments, we would see a health revolution, and recovery rates and miracles like we've never seen before.

Magic Practice Number 4

Magical Health

1. Repeat steps one to three of Magic Practice Number 1 – Count Your Blessings: Make a list of ten blessings. Write *why* you're grateful. Reread your list, say *thank you, thank you, thank you,* and feel gratitude for each one.

2. On a piece of paper or card write the words: **THE GIFT OF HEALTH IS KEEPING ME ALIVE.**

3. Place the piece of paper with your written words where you know you will see it often today.

4. On at least **four** occasions, read the words very slowly, and feel as grateful as you can for the precious gift of health!

5. Just before you go to sleep tonight, hold your Magic Rock in one hand, and say the magic words, *thank you,* for the *best* thing that happened during the day.

Day 5
MAGIC MONEY

"Gratitude is riches. Complaint is poverty."

If there's a lack of money in your life, understand that feeling worried, envious, jealous, disappointed, discouraged, doubtful, or fearful about money can never bring more money to you, because those feelings come from a lack of gratitude for the money you have. Complaining about money, arguing about money, getting frustrated about money, being critical of the cost of something, or making someone else feel bad about money are not acts of gratitude, and the money in your life can never improve; it will worsen.

No matter what your current situation, the very thought that you don't have enough money is being ungrateful for the money you have. You have to get your current situation out of your mind and instead feel grateful for the money you do have, so the money in your life can magically increase!

*"Whoever has **gratitude** (for money) will be given more, and she or he will have an abundance. Whoever does not have **gratitude** (for money), even what she or he has will be taken from her or him."*

Feeling grateful for money when you have very little is challenging for anyone, but when you understand that nothing will change until you're grateful you will be inspired to do it.

The subject of money can be a tricky one for many people, especially when they don't have enough, so there are two steps to the Magic Money practice. It's important that you read through the entire practice of Magic Money at the beginning of the day, because you will continue with the money practice throughout the day.

Sit down and take a few minutes to think back through your childhood before you had any or much money. As you recall each memory where money was paid *for* you, say and feel the magic words, *thank you,* with all your heart for each instance.

Did you always have food to eat?

Did you live in a home?

Did you receive an education over many years?

How did you travel to school each day? Did you have schoolbooks, school lunches, and all the things you needed for school?

Did you go on any vacations when you were a child?

What were the most exciting birthday gifts you received when you were a child?

Did you have a bike, toys, or a pet?

Did you have clothes as you grew so quickly from one size to the next?

Did you go to the movies, play sports, learn a musical instrument, or pursue a hobby?

Did you go to the doctor and take medicine when you were not well?

Did you go to the dentist?

Did you have essential items that you used every day, like your toothbrush, toothpaste, soap, and shampoo?

Did you travel in a car?

Did you watch television, make phone calls, use lights, electricity, and water?

All of these things cost money, and you received them all – at no charge! As you travel back through memories of your childhood and youth, you'll realize how many things you received that equate to hard earned money. Be grateful for every single instance and memory, because when you can feel sincere gratitude for the money you've received in the past, your money will magically increase in the future! It is guaranteed by Universal law.

To continue with the practice of Magic Money, take a dollar bill and write on a sticker that you place on the bill:

THANK YOU FOR ALL THE MONEY I'VE BEEN GIVEN THROUGHOUT MY LIFE.

Take your Magic Dollar Bill with you today and put it in your wallet, purse, or pocket. At least once in the morning and once in the afternoon, or as many times as you want, take it out and hold the Magic Dollar Bill in your hands. Read your written words and be *truly* grateful for the abundance of money you've been given in your life. The more sincere you are, and the more you feel it, the faster you will see a miraculous change to the circumstances of your money.

You will never know ahead of time how your money will increase, but likely you will see many different circumstances change for you to have more money. You could find money you didn't realize you had, receive unexpected cash or checks, receive discounts, rebates, or decreases in costs, or receive all kinds of material things that would have cost you money.

After today, put your Magic Dollar Bill in a place where you will continue to see it every day to remind you to be grateful for the abundance of money you have been given, never forgetting that the more times you look at your Magic Dollar Bill and feel gratitude for the money you have been given, the more magic you will bring forth. An abundance of gratitude for money equals an abundance of money!

If you find yourself in a situation where you're about to complain about something to do with money, whether it's through your words or your thoughts, ask yourself: "Am I willing to pay the price for this complaint?" Because that one complaint will slow or even stop the flow of money.

From this day forward, make a promise to yourself that whenever you receive any money, whether it's your salary for work, a refund or discount, or something that someone gives you that costs money, you will be truly grateful for it. Each of these circumstances means that you have received money, and each instance gives you an opportunity to use gratitude's magical power to increase and multiply your money even more by being grateful for the money you've just received!

Magic Practice Number 5

Magic Money

1. Repeat steps one to three of Magic Practice Number 1 – Count Your Blessings: Make a list of ten blessings. Write *why* you're grateful. Reread your list, say *thank you, thank you, thank you,* and feel gratitude for each one.

2. Sit down and take a few minutes to think back through your childhood and all the things you received that were provided at no charge to you.

3. As you recall each memory where money was paid *for* you, say and feel the magic words, *thank you,* with all your heart for each instance.

4. Take a dollar bill or other small bill and write on a sticker that you place on the bill in big bold letters:

    THANK YOU FOR ALL THE MONEY I'VE BEEN GIVEN THROUGHOUT MY LIFE.

5. Take your Magic Dollar Bill with you today, and at least once in the morning and once in the afternoon, or as many times as you want, take it out and hold the Magic Dollar Bill in your hands. Read your written words and be *truly* grateful for the abundance of money you've been given.

6. After today, put your Magic Dollar Bill somewhere you will see it every day to remind you to continue to be grateful for the abundance of money you have been given in your life.

7. Just before you go to sleep tonight, hold your Magic Rock in one hand, and say the magic words, *thank you,* for the *best* thing that happened during the day.

Day 6
WORKS LIKE MAGIC

"If you take any activity, any art, any discipline,
any skill - take it and push it as far as it will go,
push it beyond where it has ever been before, push
it to the wildest edges of edges, then you force it into
the realm of magic."

TOM ROBBINS (B. 1936)
WRITER

How can it be that a person who is born into total poverty, starts out with nothing, and has very little education goes on to become a president or a celebrity, or builds an empire and becomes one of the wealthiest people in the world? And how is it that two people can start out in the same career, and yet one person's career goes from success to even greater success, while the other person works himself or herself into the ground, with little success, no matter how hard they try? The missing link to success is gratitude, because according to the law of attraction you have to be grateful for what you have to attract success to you. So, without gratitude, it's impossible to have permanent success.

To bring success or increase the good things in your job or work, like opportunities, promotions, money, brilliant ideas, inspirations, and appreciation, it is essential to be grateful for your job or work. The more gratitude you have, the more you will have to be grateful for! And you should be getting the idea by now that to increase anything in your life, you have to be grateful for what you already have.

*"Whoever has **gratitude** (for their work) will be given more, and he or she will have an abundance. Whoever does not have **gratitude** (for their work), even what he or she has will be taken from him or her."*

When you are grateful for your job, you will automatically give more to your work, and when you give more to your work, you will increase the money and success that is returned to you. If you are not grateful for your job, you will automatically give less. When you give less you decrease what comes back to you, and as a result, you will never be happy in your work, you will never give more than you have to, and your job or work will stagnate and eventually deteriorate, which could mean losing your job. Remember, for those who do not have gratitude, even what they have will be taken from them.

The amount you give in gratitude is exactly proportional to the amount you receive in return.

You control the amount you receive, by the amount of gratitude you give!

If you are a business owner, your business's value will increase or decrease according to your gratitude. The more grateful you are for your business, your customers, and your employees, the more the business will grow and increase. It is when business owners stop being grateful and replace gratitude with worry that their business spirals downward.

If you're a parent and your work is taking care of your children and managing your home, look for the things to be grateful for at this time in your life. It is often a once-in-a-lifetime opportunity, and when you can be grateful for this time, you will attract more support, more help, more beautiful moments, and more happiness to the experience.

You should love your job, whatever it is, and be excited about going to work, and you shouldn't settle for anything less. If you don't feel that way about your current job, or if it's not your dream job, the way to receive your dream job is by first being grateful for the job you have.

Today, imagine that you have an invisible manager whose job it is to keep a record of the thoughts and feelings you have about your job. Imagine that your manager will follow you wherever you go today, poised with pen and notebook in hand. Every time you find something about your job to be grateful for, your manager will make a note of it. Your job is to find as many things as you can to be grateful for so at the end of the day your manager has a long list of all your gratitude. The longer the list is, the more magic your invisible manager can bring to your money, work success, opportunities, enjoyment, and fulfillment.

Think about all the things you could be grateful for in your work. To begin with, think about the fact that you actually have a job! Think about how many people are unemployed, who would give *anything* to have a job. Think about the timesaving equipment you use, such as phones, printers, the Internet, and computers. Think about the people you work with, and the friendships you have with them. Think about the people who make your job easier, such as receptionists, assistants, janitors, and delivery people. Think about how good it feels when you receive your paycheck, and think about the favorite aspects of your job that you love doing.

Have your invisible manager make a note each time you find something you're grateful for, by saying:

I'm so grateful for _____*what?*_____ .

The more deeply your manager can see you're feeling gratitude, the sooner your manager can start to make the magic happen in your work, and the more magic will be created. It is possible that you could generate so much gratitude for your work in one day that you would see the circumstances instantly improve. Lucky breaks don't happen by accident. They are simply gratitude's magical power at work!

If this Works Like Magic practice falls on a weekend or when you're not at work, move on to the next day's practice or practices, and then go back and use this magical practice on the first day you're back at work.

Magic Practice Number 6

Works Like Magic

1. Repeat steps one to three of Magic Practice Number 1 – Count Your Blessings: Make a list of ten blessings. Write *why* you're grateful. Reread your list, say *thank you, thank you, thank you,* and feel gratitude for each one.

2. While at work today, imagine you have an invisible manager following you around taking notes every time you find something to be grateful for. Your job today is to look for as many things as you can to be grateful for.

3. Have your manager make a note each time you find something you're grateful for, by saying: *I'm so grateful for _____what?_____*, and feel as grateful as you can.

4. Just before you go to sleep tonight, hold your Magic Rock in one hand, and say the magic words, *thank you,* for the *best* thing that happened during the day.

Day 7
THE MAGICAL WAY OUT OF NEGATIVITY

"A thankful person is thankful under all circumstances."

BAHÁ'U'LLÁH (1817–1892)
PERSIAN FOUNDER OF THE BAHÁ'Í FAITH

Whether it's a relationship in turmoil, financial pressure, a lack of health, or problems in a job, negative situations arise because of a lack of gratitude over a long period of time. If we are not grateful for each thing in our lives, we are unintentionally taking those things for granted. Taking things for granted is a major cause of negativity, because when we *take* things for granted we are not *giving* thanks in return, and we stop the magic happening in our life. Just as giving thanks to others will always lead to our life magically increasing, so must taking things for granted always lead to our life decreasing.

Are you grateful for your health when it's good? Or do you only notice your health when your body gets sick or hurts? Are you grateful for your job every day, or do you only value your job when you hear there will be cutbacks? Are you grateful for your pay or salary every single time you receive it, or do you take your pay or salary for granted? Are you grateful for your loved ones when everything is running smoothly, or do you only talk to others about your loved ones when there are problems? Are you grateful when your car is working well? Or do you only think of your car when it breaks down?

Are you grateful to be alive each day? Or do you take your life for granted?

Taking things for granted results in complaining, negative thoughts and words. So when you complain, by the law of attraction, you must bring more things into your life to complain about!

If you're complaining about the weather, the traffic, your boss, your spouse, your family, a friend, a stranger, waiting in lines, bills, the economy, the cost of something, or the service of a company, you are not being grateful, and you're pushing your dream life further away with every complaint.

Now you understand that complaining, negative thoughts and words, and taking things for granted stops the good things in your life. Now you understand that when something goes very wrong you have unintentionally not been grateful enough.

It's impossible to be negative when you're grateful. It's impossible to criticize and blame when you're grateful. It's impossible to feel sad or have any negative feeling when you're grateful. And the best news is that if you have any negative situations in your life currently, it won't take a long period of time to transform them with gratitude. The negative situations will disappear in a puff of smoke – just like magic!

First, as difficult as it may be, you have to look for things to be grateful for in the negative situation. No matter how bad things are, you can always find something to be grateful for, especially when you know that your gratitude will magically transform every negative circumstance. Walt Disney, who knew about the true magic of life, showed us how to do this in his movie *Pollyanna*.

Disney's 1960 movie *Pollyanna* featured "The Glad Game," which had a profound effect on me when I was a child. I played The Glad Game featured in the movie through my childhood and adolescence. To play The Glad Game, you look for as many things as you can to be glad about, especially in a negative situation. Finding things to be glad about (or finding things to be grateful for) in a negative situation make the solutions appear!

Walt Disney demonstrated the magical power of gratitude in *Pollyanna*, and thousands of years earlier Buddha demonstrated the way to use the same magical power when he said:

"Let us rise up and be thankful, for if we didn't learn a lot today, at least we learned a little, and if we didn't learn a little, at least we didn't get sick, and if we got sick, at least we didn't die; so, let us all be thankful."

GAUTAMA BUDDHA (CIRCA 563 BC–483 BC)
FOUNDER OF BUDDHISM

Let Buddha's words be your inspiration, and today take one problem or negative situation in your life that you most want to resolve, and look for ten things to be grateful for. I know it can be challenging to begin this practice, but Buddha is showing you the way to do it. Make a written list of ten things on your computer, or in your gratitude journal.

As an example, your problem might be that you're out of work, and despite your best efforts, you're still unemployed. To magically turn this situation around, you have to do a concentrated practice of gratitude on the situation. Here are some examples of what you might say:

1. *I am so grateful to have had more time for my family during this period.*

2. *I'm grateful that my life is in a lot better order because of the spare time I've had.*

3. *I am grateful that I've had a job most of my life, and that I am experienced.*

4. *I am truly grateful that this is the first time I've been unemployed.*

5. *I'm grateful that there are jobs out there, and more new jobs are appearing each day.*

6. *I am grateful for all the things I've learned in applying for jobs and in going for interviews.*

7. *I am grateful that I have my health and that I can work.*

8. *I'm grateful for my family's encouragement and support.*

9. *I'm grateful for the rest I've had, because I needed it.*

10. *I'm grateful that through losing my job, I've realized how much having a job means to me. I had never realized that until now.*

As a result of the unemployed person's gratitude, they will attract different circumstances, and their current situation must and will magically change. The power of gratitude is greater than any negative situation, and there are unlimited ways that the negative situation can change. All you have to do is practice gratitude and watch the magic take place!

Let's take another example; a son whose relationship with his father is troubled. The son feels that no matter what he does it never seems to be good enough for his father.

1. *I am grateful that most of the relationships in my life are really good.*

2. *I'm grateful to my father for working hard so that I could have the education that he didn't get to have.*

3. *I'm grateful to my father for supporting our family through my childhood, because I didn't have a clue then how much hard work and money it took to keep our family going.*

4. *I'm grateful to my father for taking me to basketball every Saturday when I was a child.*

5. *I'm grateful that my father is not as tough on me these days as he used to be in the past.*

6. *I'm grateful that my father cares so much about me, because he wouldn't be tough if he didn't care so much.*

7. *I'm grateful that through my relationship with my father I have learned to have compassion and a greater understanding with my children.*

8. *I'm grateful to my father for showing me how important encouragement is in raising happy, confident children.*

9. *I'm really grateful when I get to laugh with my father. Some people never got to do that because they didn't have a father. And for others, who have lost their father, they will never have the chance to laugh with their father again.*

10. *I am so truly grateful that I have my father, because amid the tough times, there have been good times, and there will be more good times ahead with my father.*

As a result of the son's heartfelt feelings of gratitude for his father, he will change their relationship for the better. The son changed the way he thinks and feels about his father, which immediately changes what he attracts from his father. Even though the son was being grateful in his mind, at an energetic and quantum level, the son's gratitude will have a magical effect on his relationship with his father. Provided he maintains his gratitude, by the law of attraction, the son must receive far better circumstances with his father, and their relationship must begin to improve immediately.

Remember, you can tell your gratitude is working by the way that you feel. You should feel a lot better about the situation after practicing gratitude. The first evidence of gratitude's magical power working is your feelings lifting, so when you do feel better about it, you know the situation will improve and the solutions will appear. The answer to any negative situation you want to resolve is to focus concentrated gratitude on it until you feel better inside; then you will see the magic work its wonder in the outside world.

In making your written list, make sure you list each of the ten things you're grateful for in the following way:

I am so grateful for _____.
Or, *I am truly grateful for* _____.

And finish the sentence with what you're grateful for. You can also use Walt Disney's way of using gratitude's magical power if you find it easier:

I am so glad that _____.

And finish the sentence with what you're glad about.

Once you've listed ten things you're grateful for, finish the Magical Way Out of Negativity practice by writing:

Thank you, thank you, thank you, for the perfect resolution.

And just for today, see if you can get through one day without saying anything negative. It may be a challenge, but see if you can make it through *one* day. There is an important reason to do this, because most of us have no idea how much we speak negatively, but you'll have an idea after watching your words for a day. Remember that negativity and complaint bring more of those things, and if you're aware of what you're saying you can stop and decide if you want the consequences of what you're about to say. Here is a magic lifeline you can use if you notice yourself thinking or saying something negative. Stop immediately, and say:

But I have to say that I am really grateful for _____.

Finish the rest of the sentence with something – anything – that you're grateful for. Take this magic lifeline with you, and grab a hold of it whenever you need it.

And if any little problem or situation appears in the future, remember to put out the embers with gratitude before it grows into a fire. At the same time you will ignite the magic in your life!

MAGIC PRACTICE NUMBER 7

The Magical Way Out of Negativity

1. Count Your Blessings: Make a list of ten blessings. Write *why* you're grateful. Reread your list, and at the end of each blessing say *thank you, thank you, thank you,* and feel as grateful for that blessing as you can.

2. Choose one problem or negative situation in your life that you most want to resolve.

3. List **ten** things that you are grateful for about the negative situation.

4. At the end of your list, write:
    Thank you, thank you, thank you, for the perfect resolution.

5. Just for today, see if you can get through one day without saying anything negative. If you notice yourself thinking or saying something negative, use the magic lifeline. Stop immediately and say:
    But I have to say that I am really grateful for _____.

6. Just before you go to sleep tonight, hold your Magic Rock in one hand, and say the magic words, *thank you,* for the *best* thing that happened during the day.

Day 8
THE MAGIC INGREDIENT

"A thankful heart hath a continual feast."

W. J. CAMERON (1879–1953)
JOURNALIST AND BUSINESSMAN

Giving thanks for food before you eat is a tradition that has been followed for thousands of years, dating back to the ancient Egyptians. With the fast pace of life in the twenty-first century, taking the time to give thanks for a meal has more often than not been left behind. But using the simple act of eating and drinking as an opportunity to be grateful will increase the magic in your life exponentially!

If you think about a time when you were really hungry, you will remember that you could not think or function normally, your body felt weak, you might have started to tremble, your mind became confused, and your feelings plummeted. All of this can happen after not eating for just a few hours! You need food to live, to think, and to feel good, and so there is a *great* deal to be grateful for about food.

To feel even more gratitude for food, take a moment and think about all the people who contributed to you having food to eat. For you to eat fresh fruit and vegetables, the growers had to plant and nurture the fruit and vegetables with continuous watering, protecting them over many months until they were ready for harvesting. Then there are the pickers, the packers, and the distributors, and the transportation people who drive enormous distances day and night, all of them working together in perfect harmony to ensure that every fruit and vegetable is delivered fresh to you, and is available year round.

Think about the meat growers, fishermen, dairy farmers, coffee and tea growers, and all the packaged food companies who work tirelessly to produce the food we eat. The world's food production is a breathtaking orchestration that takes place every day, and it's unfathomable that it all works when you think about the number of people involved in maintaining the world's food and drink supplies to stores, restaurants, supermarkets, cafés, airplanes, schools, hospitals, and every home on the planet.

Food is a gift! It's a gift of nature, because there would be nothing for any of us to eat if nature didn't supply us with the soil, nutrients, and water to grow food. Without water, there would be no food, vegetation, animals, or human life. We use water to cook our meals, grow our food, maintain our gardens, supply our bathrooms, sustain every vehicle that moves, support our hospitals, fuel, mining, and manufacturing industries, enable transportation, make our roads, make clothes and every consumer product and appliance on the planet, make plastic, glass, and metal, make life-saving medications, and build our homes and every other building and structure. And water keeps our bodies alive. Water, water, water, glorious water!

> *"If there is magic on this planet it is contained in water."*
>
> LOREN EISELEY (1907–1977)
> ANTHROPOLOGIST AND NATURAL SCIENCE WRITER

Where would we be without food and water? We simply wouldn't be here. None of our family or friends would be here either. We wouldn't have this day, or any tomorrow. But here we are on this beautiful planet together, living life with its challenges and ecstatic joys, because of nature's gifts of *food* and *water!* To say the simple, magic words, *thank you,* before you eat or drink anything is an act of recognition and gratitude for the miracle of food and water.

The incredible thing is that when you are grateful for food and water, it doesn't just affect your life; your gratitude also impacts the world's supply. If enough people felt gratitude for food and water, it would actually help the people who are starving and in great need. By the law of the attraction, and Newton's law of action and reaction, the action of mass gratitude must produce an equal mass reaction, which would change the circumstances of scarcity of food and water for everyone on the planet.

In addition, your gratitude for food and water keeps the magic continuing in *your* life, and it will weave its glorious golden thread through everything that is dear to you, everything that you love, and everything that you're dreaming of.

In ancient times people believed that when they blessed their food and water with gratitude it purified whatever they were blessing, and when you look at the theories and discoveries that quantum physics have made in recent times, such as the observer effect, the ancients may very well have been right. The observer effect in quantum physics refers to changes that the act of observation makes on whatever is being observed. Imagine if focusing gratitude on your food and drinks changed their energy structure, and purified them so that everything you consumed had the ultimate effect of well-being on your body?

One of the ways to experience the magic of gratitude instantly with food and drinks is to really savor what you're eating or drinking. When you savor your food or drinks you're appreciating them, or being grateful. As an experiment, next time you're in the middle of eating food or drinking any liquid, when you take a mouthful, concentrate on the taste of the food in your mouth or the flavor of the liquid before you swallow it. You'll find that when you focus on the food or drink in your mouth, and savor it, the flavors seem to explode, and when you don't focus the flavors weaken dramatically.

It's your energy of focus and gratitude that instantly enhances the flavor!

Before you eat or drink anything today, whether you're about to eat a meal, a piece of fruit, or a snack, or have a drink of anything, including water, take a moment to look at what you're about to eat or drink, and in your mind or out loud say the magic words, *thank you!* And if you can, just take one mouthful really savoring it; it will not only increase your enjoyment, it will help you to feel far more gratitude.

You can also try something I do, which helps me to feel even more gratitude. When I say the magic words, I wave my fingers over my food or drink as though I'm sprinkling them with magic dust, and I imagine that the magic dust instantly purifies everything it touches. Doing this has helped me really feel that gratitude is the magic ingredient, and I want to add it to everything I eat and drink! If you find it more effective you can imagine that you have a shaker of magic dust in your hand, and you're shaking the magic dust out of the shaker all over your food before you eat it, and into every drink.

If at any time during the day you forget to say the magic words, *thank you,* before you eat or drink anything, as soon as you remember, close your eyes, go back in your mind to the time when you forgot, visualize yourself in your mind for a second or two before you ate or drank, and say the magic words. If you forget to be grateful for food and drinks multiple times in the day, then repeat this same practice tomorrow. You can't afford to miss a single day in building your gratitude – your dreams depend upon it!

Being grateful for the simple things in life, like food and water, is one of the deepest expressions of gratitude, and when you can feel that degree of gratitude, you will see the magic happen.

MAGIC PRACTICE NUMBER 8

The Magic Ingredient

1. Count Your Blessings: Make a list of ten blessings. Write *why* you're grateful. Reread your list, and at the end of each blessing say *thank you, thank you, thank you,* and feel as grateful for that blessing as you can.

2. Before you eat or drink anything today, take a moment to look at what you're about to eat or drink, and in your mind or out loud, say the magic words, *thank you!* If you want you can sprinkle your food or drink with magic dust.

3. Just before you go to sleep tonight, hold your Magic Rock in one hand, and say the magic words, *thank you,* for the *best* thing that happened during the day.

Day 9
THE MONEY MAGNET

"It is only with gratitude that life becomes rich."

DIETRICH BONHOEFFER (1906–1945)
LUTHERAN PASTOR

Gratitude is riches and complaint is poverty; it's
the golden rule of your whole life, whether it's your
health, job, relationships, or money. The more grateful
you can be for the money you have, even if you don't
have very much, the more riches you will receive. And
the more you complain about money, the poorer you
will become.

Today's magical practice turns one of the biggest
reasons people complain about money into an act of
gratitude, and so it has double the power to change
the circumstances of your money; you'll be *replacing*
a complaint, which makes you poorer, with gratitude,
which magically brings you riches.

Most people wouldn't think they complain about
money, but if there is a lack of money in their life they

are complaining without realizing it. Complaining happens through people's thoughts as well as their words, and most people aren't aware of the many thoughts in their head. Any complaining, negative, jealous, or worried thoughts or words about money are literally creating poverty. And of course the biggest complaints come when money has to be paid out.

If you don't have enough money, paying your bills can be one of the most difficult things to do. It can seem like there is a greater stream of bills than there is money to pay them. But if you complain about your bills then what you are really doing is complaining about money, and complaining keeps you in poverty.

If you don't have enough money, the last thing you would normally do is feel grateful for your bills, but in fact that's exactly what you *have* to do to receive more money in your life. To have a rich life, you must be grateful for everything to do with money, and begrudging your bills is not being grateful. You must do the exact opposite, which is to *be grateful* for the goods or services you've *received* from those who billed you. It is such a simple thing to do, but it will have a monumental effect on the money in your life. You will literally become a money magnet!

To be grateful for a bill, think about how much you've benefited from the service or goods on the bill. If it's payment for rent or a mortgage, be grateful that you have a home, and you're living in it. What if the only way you could live in a home was by saving up all the money and paying cash for it? What if there was no such thing as lending institutions or places to rent? Most of us would be living on the streets, so be grateful to the lending institutions or your landlord, because they have made it possible for you to live in a home or apartment.

If you're paying a bill for gas or electricity, think about the heating or cooling you received, the hot showers, and every appliance you were able to use because of the service. If you're paying a phone or Internet bill, imagine how difficult your life would be if you had to travel vast distances to talk to each person individually. Think about how many times you've been able to call family and friends, send and receive emails, or access information instantly through the Internet because of your service provider. All of these remarkable services are at your fingertips, so be grateful for them, and be grateful that the companies trust you by providing their services *before* you have paid for them.

Ever since I discovered the phenomenal power of gratitude, I write the magic words, "*Thank you – Paid,*" on every bill as I pay it, and I never miss a single one. At the beginning, when I didn't have the money to pay a bill, I would still use gratitude's magical power, and would instead write across the bill, "*Thank you for the money.*" Then when I had the money to pay it, I would add, "*Thank you – Paid.*"

Today you are going to do the same. Take any currently unpaid bills you have, and use gratitude's magical power by writing across them, "*Thank you for the money,*" and feel grateful for having the money to pay the bill, whether you have it or not. If you receive and pay most of your bills online, then when you receive an online bill forward it to yourself as an email and write in the subject line in capital bold letters, **THANK YOU FOR THE MONEY.**

Next, find ten bills you've paid in the past and write across the front of each one the magic words, "*Thank you – Paid.*" As you write on each paid bill, feel as grateful as you possibly can that you had the money to pay the bill. The more gratitude you can harness for the bills you've paid, the more money you will magically magnetize to you!   •

From this day forward, you could make it your regular practice that whenever you pay a bill, you briefly think about the great service you've received from the bill, and write across the face of the bill the magic words, "*Thank you – Paid.*" And if you don't have the money to pay a bill, use gratitude's magical power and write, "*Thank you for the money,*" and feel as if you're saying thank you because you *have* the money to pay the bill!

Feeling gratitude for the money you've paid out guarantees you will receive more. Gratitude is like a magnetic golden thread attached to your money, so when you pay money out, the money always returns to you, sometimes equally, sometimes tenfold, sometimes a hundredfold. The abundance you receive back depends not on how much money you give, but on how much gratitude you give. You could have so much gratitude when you pay a bill for fifty dollars that you could receive back hundreds of dollars.

Magic Practice Number 9

The Money Magnet

1. Count Your Blessings: Make a list of ten blessings. Write *why* you're grateful. Reread your list, and at the end of each blessing say *thank you, thank you, thank you,* and feel as grateful for that blessing as you can.

2. Take any current unpaid bills you have, use gratitude's magical power, and write across each one: *Thank you for the money.* Feel grateful for having the money to pay the bill, whether you have it or not.

3. Take **ten** bills you've paid in the past, and write across the front of each one of them the magic words: "*Thank you – Paid.*" Feel truly grateful that you had the money to pay the bill!

4. Before you go to sleep, take your Magic Rock in one hand, and say the magic words, *thank you,* for the *best* thing that happened during the day.

Day 10
MAGIC DUST EVERYONE

*"No duty is more urgent than that
of returning thanks."*

SAINT AMBROSE (AD 340–397)
THEOLOGIAN AND CATHOLIC BISHOP

Ancient spiritual teachings say that what we give
to another person with a full heart returns to us a
hundredfold. So being grateful and saying *thank you* to
another person for anything you receive from them is
not only urgent, it's vital to improving *your* life!

Gratitude is a powerful energy, and so whomever you
direct gratitude's energy toward, that's where it goes. If
you think of gratitude's energy looking like sparkling
magic dust, then when you express gratitude to another
person in return for something you've received from
them, you are literally sprinkling them with that magic
dust! The powerful, positive energy in magic dust
reaches and affects whomever you sprinkle it on.

Most of us make contact with many people every day, whether on the phone, through email, or face to face at work, in stores, restaurants, elevators, buses, or trains, and in many cases the people we make contact with deserve our gratitude, because we are receiving something from them.

Think about the people you encounter on a typical day who provide you with some kind of service, like those working in stores or restaurants, bus or cab drivers, customer service people, cleaners, or the staff at your work. The people who work in service are *giving themselves* to serve you, and you're *receiving* their service. If you don't say *thank you* in return for their service, then you're not being grateful, and you're stopping the good from coming into your life.

Think about the maintenance workers who keep our transport systems working safely, and those who maintain the service of utilities such as electricity, gas, water, and our roads.

Think about the cleaners of the world who clean our streets, public bathrooms, trains, buses, airplanes, hospitals, restaurants, supermarkets, and office buildings. You can't personally say *thank you* to all of them, but you can sprinkle them with magic dust by saying *thank you* next time you pass one of them. And you can be grateful next time you sit at your clean desk, or walk on a clean sidewalk, or across a polished floor.

When you're at a café or restaurant, sprinkle magic dust by saying *thank you* to each person as they serve you. Whether cleaning the table, giving you the menu, receiving your order, filling your glass with water, serving the meal you ordered, clearing the table, giving you the bill, or giving your change, remember to say *thank you* every single time. If you're in a store or supermarket checkout, sprinkle magic dust and say *thank you* to the person who serves you or packs your groceries.

If you are traveling by plane, sprinkle magic dust by saying *thank you* to the check-in people, the people in security, the person who checks your ticket as you board, and the cabin crew who greet you as you enter the plane. During the flight, say *thank you* to the cabin crew every time they perform a service for you. Serving drinks and food or removing your plate or trash is a service. The airline thanks you for flying with them, the captain thanks you, and the crew thank you, so do the same and thank *them* as you leave the plane. And every time you take off and land at your destination say *thank you,* because the fact that you can fly is an absolute miracle!

Be grateful to those people who assist you in your work, whether they are clerical staff, receptionists, canteen staff, cleaners, customer service people, or any of your work colleagues. Magic dust them all with *thank you!* All of them are doing you a service, and they deserve your continued gratitude in return.

Store assistants, waiters, and waitresses work very hard to serve people. They have chosen a job to serve other people, and serving the public means encountering all kinds of people in varying moods, including those who are ungrateful. Next time you are being served by another person, remember that the person who is serving you is a precious daughter or son to parents, an irreplaceable brother or sister to siblings, a mother or father to a family and children, and a loved and adored partner or friend, and they deserve your kindness and patience.

At times you may encounter a person in service who behaves rudely toward you or doesn't give you the attention you think you deserve. It may be more challenging to be grateful in these situations, but your gratitude cannot be dependent on another person's behavior. Choose to be grateful no matter what! Choose magic in your life no matter what! It might help you to remember that you don't know what difficulty someone might be going through at the time you connect with him or her. They may be feeling unwell, they may have just lost a loved one, their marriage might have just ended, or they may be in desperation and at a tipping point in their life. Your gratitude and kindness might be the most magical thing that happens to them that day.

> *"Be kind, for everyone you meet is fighting a hard battle."*
>
> PHILO OF ALEXANDRIA (CIRCA 20 BC–AD 50)
> PHILOSOPHER

If you thank someone on the phone for his or her help, don't throw away your *thank you;* instead, give the reason *why* you're grateful. For example, "Thank you for your help." "Thank you for going out of your way for me." "Thank you for giving me so much of your time." "Thank you for resolving the situation for me, I'm very grateful to you." You will be amazed at the response from the other person when you do this one simple thing, because they will feel your sincerity.

When you say *thank you* to someone in person, look at his or her face. They will not feel your gratitude or receive your magic dust unless you look directly at them. You've wasted an opportunity to help that person and to change your own life if you say *thank you* to the air, or say *thank you* as you're looking down, or *thank you* while you're on your cell phone, because you're not really sincere when you do that.

A couple of years ago I was in a store buying a gift for my sister. The store assistant who served me listened to what I was looking for, and then went on a search for the perfect gift as though it was for *her* sister! As the store assistant handed me the bag containing the perfect, beautifully wrapped gift, I received a call on my cell phone. I was finishing the call when I reached the front entrance of the store, and suddenly an unsettled feeling swept over me. I immediately returned to the store assistant who had helped me, and I not only thanked her, but I told her all the reasons *why* I was grateful to her, and how much I appreciated everything she did for me. I showered her with gratitude's magic dust! Her eyes filled with tears, and the biggest smile you've ever seen swept across her face.

Every action always has an equal reaction. If you really mean it when you say *thank you,* the other person will feel it, and you will not only have made another person feel really good, but your gratitude will fill *you* with an indescribable happiness. That day I walked out of the store indescribably happy.

I don't use magic dust only for the people who serve; I use gratitude's magic dust in all kinds of situations. When I say goodbye to my daughter before she drives to her home, I feel gratitude for her having arrived home safely, and I wave my fingers in the air and imagine sprinkling magic dust over her and her car. Sometimes I sprinkle magic dust on my computer before I begin a new project, or sprinkle magic dust ahead of me before I walk into a store to look for something in particular that I need. My daughter uses magic dust when she's driving, and if she sees another driver who seems to be stressed and is speeding, she sprinkles magic dust over them to help make them feel better and keep them safe.

Today, take gratitude's magic dust with you for the people who work in service, and look for every opportunity you can to sprinkle magic dust on everyone by saying *thank you.* Thank at least ten people who perform different services you benefit from today. It doesn't matter if you don't get the opportunity to do it in person; you can mentally acknowledge the people whose service you benefit from. The magic dust will still reach them. As an example, mentally say to yourself:

*I'm really grateful to the cleaners who work through the early
hours of the morning, making sure that the streets are cleaned
of trash every day. I've never really thought about how grateful
I am for that service, which is done like clockwork every day.
Thank you.*

Make sure you keep count of the people in service
you are grateful for, so that you know when you have
thanked ten different people for their services and
sprinkled magic dust on them all. If you imagine the
sparkling magic dust falling over people when you
thank them, you have a picture of what really happens
in the invisible with the power of gratitude. With this
picture in your mind, it will help you to believe and
know that the magic dust of gratitude really does reach
people, and that it will be available to help them to
improve their lives. And every time you sprinkle magic
dust over another person, it also returns to you in your
own life.

If you're at home today, then sit down with a pen and
journal or on your computer, and go back in your
mind recalling instances where people in service went
out of their way for you. It may have been someone on
the phone, or it may have been a tradesperson who
was determined to resolve a problem for you. Maybe
you've received great service from your mail person, the
trash collectors or recycling companies, or local store
assistants. Make a written list of ten instances where
people in service helped you, and send magic dust by
saying *thank you* to every one of them.

Magic Reminder

Read through tomorrow's practice today, because the practice for Day 11 begins when you first wake up.

Magic Practice Number 10

Magic Dust Everyone

1. Count Your Blessings: Make a list of ten blessings. Write *why* you're grateful. Reread your list, and at the end of each blessing say *thank you, thank you, thank you,* and feel as grateful for that blessing as you can.

2. Today, sprinkle magic dust on **ten** people who perform services you benefit from, by thanking them directly or otherwise by mentally acknowledging and thanking them. Feel grateful to them for the service they perform!

3. Just before you go to sleep tonight, hold your Magic Rock in one hand, and say the magic words, *thank you,* for the *best* thing that happened during the day.

4. Read through tomorrow's practice today, because the practice for Day 11 begins when you first wake up.

Day 11
A MAGIC MORNING

"When you arise in the morning think of what a privilege it is to be alive, to think, to enjoy, to love."

MARCUS AURELIUS (121–180)
ROMAN EMPEROR

The easiest and simplest way to ensure that your day ahead will be filled with *magic* is to fill your *morning* with gratitude. When you incorporate gratitude into your morning routine, you will feel and see its magical benefits throughout the whole day.

Each morning is full of opportunities to give thanks, and it doesn't slow you down or take any extra time, because you can do it naturally as you go about everything you do. There is an added bonus to filling your morning with gratitude because your daily routines are the times when you can harm yourself the most by thinking negative thoughts without realizing you're doing it. There's no room for harmful negative thoughts when your mind is focused on looking for things to be grateful for. After this practice you will go into your day feeling much happier and more confident that the day ahead will be great – and that's when you will see the magic happen before your very eyes!

When you wake up to the new day today, before you move, before you do a single thing, say the magic words, *thank you*. Say *thank you* for the fact that you are alive, and that you've been given another day of life. Your life is a gift, every day is a gift, and when you really think about it, it's inconceivable that any of us would wake up in the morning without giving thanks for another day. If you think a new day isn't such a big deal, then just try missing one! It doesn't matter how sleepy you are, or if your alarm has woken you up for work, or you've slept in during the weekend; the moment you wake, say the magic words, *thank you*, for another day of your life.

Say *thank you* for the good night's sleep you received. Are you fortunate enough to have slept in a bed, with sheets and a pillow? *Thank you!* As your feet hit the ground say *thank you*. Do you have a bathroom? *Thank you!* Are you able to turn on the taps and immediately receive fresh, clean water every morning? *Thank you!* Imagine all the people who dug the trenches and laid the pipes across your country, throughout your city, and along all the streets to your home so you can turn a tap and receive beautiful, clean, hot water. *Thank you!* As you reach for your toothbrush and toothpaste, *thank you!* Without them, your day would not begin so pleasantly. *Thank you* for the towels, the soap, the mirror, and everything in the bathroom you use that makes you feel fresh, awake, and ready for the day.

As you get dressed, think about how fortunate you are to have clothes to choose from and wear. *Thank you!* Think about how many people must have been involved in making all the various items of clothing you put on and wear in one day. It's likely that the clothes you put on in one day come from many countries across the planet. *Thank you to everybody!* Do you have shoes? Lucky you! Imagine life without them. *Thank you for shoes!*

> *"I have always been delighted at the prospect of a new day, a fresh try, one more start, with perhaps a bit of magic waiting somewhere behind the morning."*
>
> J. B. PRIESTLEY (1894–1984)
> WRITER AND PLAYWRIGHT

Make today as good as it can be by practicing concentrated gratitude and putting the magic into your morning routine. From the moment you open your eyes until you have put your shoes on or finished getting ready, say the magic words, *thank you,* in your mind for everything you touch and use. It doesn't matter if you don't shower or get dressed first thing in the morning, you can still use this Magic Morning practice as a guide and apply it to whatever your morning routine is. If you wake up and eat breakfast first, then as you touch and use each thing for your breakfast say the magic words, *thank you.* Give thanks for your morning coffee, tea, fruit juice, or breakfast. They make your mornings so enjoyable and give you energy for the day.

Be grateful for the kitchen appliances you use for your breakfast – the refrigerator, hot plates, oven, toaster, coffee maker, or kettle.

Every day without exception, I say "thank" as I put one foot on the floor, and "you" as my other foot touches the floor, so that as both feet touch the floor for the first time each day, I've said *thank you*. As I walk toward my bathroom I say the magic words, *thank you,* in my mind with each step. Then I continue saying *thank you* in my mind as I touch and use each thing in my bathroom. By the time I am dressed and ready for the day, I feel so happy I could jump for joy. And when I feel that happy, I know my gratitude has worked, and I am guaranteed to have a magical day. As I go through my day, I really feel as though I have a magic power with me, because one good thing after another happens. And as each good thing happens, I'm even more grateful, which speeds up the magic with even more good things happening. You know those days when everything just seems to go right for you? Well, that's what it's like after doing Magic Morning, but multiplied!

MAGIC PRACTICE NUMBER 11

A Magic Morning

1. When you wake up to the new day, before you do a single thing, say the magic words, *thank you.*

2. From the moment you open your eyes until you've finished getting ready, say the magic words, *thank you,* in your mind for everything you touch and use.

3. Count Your Blessings: Make a list of ten blessings. Write *why* you're grateful. Reread your list, and at the end of each blessing say *thank you, thank you, thank you,* and feel as grateful for that blessing as you can.

4. Just before you go to sleep tonight, hold your Magic Rock in one hand, and say the magic words, *thank you,* for the *best* thing that happened during the day.

Day 12
MAGICAL PEOPLE WHO MADE A DIFFERENCE

"At times our own light goes out and is rekindled by a spark from another person. Each one of us has cause to think with deep gratitude of those who have lighted the flame within us."

ALBERT SCHWEITZER (1875–1965)
NOBEL PEACE PRIZE–WINNING
MEDICAL MISSIONARY AND PHILOSOPHER

Every one of us has received help, support, or guidance from other people at particular times in our life when we needed it most. Sometimes another person alters the course of our life through their encouragement, guidance, or just being there at the right time. And then life goes on, and we tend to forget those times when one person touched us or changed our life. Sometimes you don't even realize the impact a person had until well into the future, when you look back on your life and realize that a particular person was pivotal in magically changing the direction of your life for the better.

The person may have been a teacher or coach, an uncle, aunt, sibling, grandparent, or any family member. They may have been a doctor, nurse, or best friend. They may have been the person who introduced you to your current partner or to a particular interest that became one of your greatest passions. Maybe they were someone you didn't even know, and they appeared in your life very briefly, performing a random act of kindness that touched you to the core.

My grandmother gave me my love for books, cooking, and the countryside. By sharing her love of those things with me, all of them affected and changed the course of my life. Cooking became a passion of mine for over twenty years, my love of books eventually led to me becoming a writer, and my love of the countryside has influenced where I've lived throughout my life.

My grandmother also disciplined me with a steel hand to say *thank you*. At the time I thought she was just teaching me to be polite. It was only later in my life I realized that teaching me to say the magic words was the greatest gift my grandmother ever gave me. She is not alive anymore, but I continue to be grateful to her for the huge influence she had on the course of my life. *Thank you, Grandma!*

Today, you are going to think about the magical people who have impacted your life. Find a quiet place alone sometime during the day today, sit down, and think of three extraordinary people who have made a difference in your life. Once you have your three people, work with one person at a time, and talk out loud to each person as though they were present, telling him or her the reasons *why* you're grateful to them, and how they affected the course of your life.

Make sure you do this magical practice with all three people in the one session, because it will take your feeling of gratitude to a far deeper level. If you split up this magical practice throughout the day, you will not feel the same depth of gratitude, nor receive the magical results.

Here's an example of what you might say:

Sarah, I want to thank you for the time that you encouraged me to follow my heart. I was lost and confused that day, and your words touched me, and lifted me out of despair. Because of what you said, I found the courage to follow my dream, and I moved to France to work as an apprentice chef. I am living my dream, and I couldn't be happier. All because of what you said to me that day. Thank you, Sarah!

It's very important that you say the reasons why you're grateful. And you can't say too much. Instead, the more you say, and the more you feel, the more amazing the results. You will see the magic explode into your life from doing this practice; it numbers among the most powerful acts of gratitude you can ever perform.

If you're not in a position to talk out loud, then you can write down your words to each person, and address them as though you're writing a letter.

When you have completed this practice, you will feel a huge difference in the way that you feel. The evidence of gratitude's power working is always that first and foremost it makes you *happy!* The secondary evidence of gratitude's power is that you attract wonderful things. And as if all of that wasn't enough, the happiness you feel after practicing gratitude also attracts more wonderful things, which will make you even happier. That's the magic of life, and that's the magical power of gratitude!

MAGIC PRACTICE NUMBER 12

Magical People Who Made a Difference

1. Count Your Blessings: Make a list of ten blessings. Write *why* you're grateful. Reread your list, and at the end of each blessing say *thank you, thank you, thank you,* and feel as grateful for that blessing as you can.

2. Find a quiet place alone sometime during today, and make a list of **three** people who made a difference in your life.

3. Work through the list one person at a time, and while talking out loud tell each person the reason why you're grateful for them, and exactly how they affected the course of your life.

4. Just before you go to sleep tonight, hold your Magic Rock in one hand, and say the magic words, *thank you,* for the *best* thing that happened during the day.

Day 13
MAKE ALL YOUR WISHES
COME TRUE

"Imagination is the true magic carpet."

NORMAN VINCENT PEALE (1898–1993)
WRITER

If you have been following the magical practices day by day, you have now built an amazing foundation by practicing gratitude for everything you have received and continue to receive in your life. But today is an exciting day, because you're going to begin to use gratitude's magical power for your dreams and desires!

Hundreds of native cultures through the centuries have traditionally given thanks for what they want *before* they receive it, creating elaborate ceremonies to put as much energy as they could into giving thanks. The Egyptians have celebrated the flooding of the Nile River since ancient times to ensure the continual flow of water in the river, American Indians and Australian Aborigines perform rain dances, various African tribes perform ceremonies for their food before they hunt for it, and the very nature of prayer in every culture and religion is giving thanks *before* having received what is desired.

The law of attraction says that like attracts like, which means you must form in your mind a likeness, or an image, of what you want. Then, to attract your desire to you, you have to feel as though it's yours, so that how you feel is also *like* how you would feel when you had what you wanted. The easiest way to do that is to be grateful for what you want – *before* you've received it. If it never occurred to you before to use gratitude to receive what you want, you have now discovered another of its magical powers. The very words in the Holy Scriptures promise exactly that:

*"Whoever has **gratitude** (now) will be given more (in the future), and he or she will have an abundance."*

Gratitude is something you must have *before* you can receive, not something that you simply do *after* something good has happened. Most people are grateful after they receive something good, but to make all your wishes come true and change your entire life by filling it with riches in every area, you must be grateful before *and* after.

Through the act of being sincerely grateful for receiving your desire *beforehand,* you immediately form an image in your mind that you have it, you feel as though you have it, and you're fulfilling your part. If you continue to hold to that image and feeling, you will magically receive your desire. You won't know how you'll receive it, and it is not your job to figure it out. You don't try to figure out how gravity is going to keep you on the ground when you go for a walk, do you? You trust and know that when you go for a walk the law of gravity will keep you firmly on the ground. Likewise, you must trust and know that when you're grateful for what you want, what you want will be magically moved to you, because it is the law of the Universe.

What Do You Most Want Right Now?

At the beginning of this book I asked you to get really clear about what you want in every area of your life. (If you didn't do that earlier, now is the time to do it.) Go to the lists you created now, and choose your top ten desires for this magical practice. You can select ten desires from different areas of your life, such as money, health, home, and relationships, or you might want to choose ten desires in one area you really want to change, such as work or success. Be very clear and specific about what you most want, so that you can see the changes magically happen from this practice. Imagine you are putting in a magic order with the Universe for your top ten desires, because in truth, by using the law of attraction, that's exactly what you are doing.

Sit down at a computer or with a pen and journal, and create a separate list of your top ten desires in the following way, *as though you've received them:*

Thank you, thank you, thank you for _____, and fill in the blank with your desire as though you've received it. For example:

Thank you, thank you, thank you for the high marks in my exam results, which got me into the exact college I wanted!

Thank you, thank you, thank you for the great news that we are having a baby!

Thank you, thank you, thank you for our dream home, which has everything we wanted it to have down to the last detail!

Thank you, thank you, thank you for the amazing phone call with my dad that has improved our relationship!

Thank you, thank you, thank you for the medical results that show I am all clear, and healthy again!

Thank you, thank you, thank you for the unexpected money I received, which is the exact amount I needed for my European trip!

Thank you, thank you, thank you for the doubling of our sales figures this month!

Thank you, thank you, thank you for the ideas that won us our biggest client yet!

Thank you, thank you, thank you for my perfect partner!

Thank you, thank you, thank you for how easy and effortless our move was!

Writing thank you three times in a row is a powerful thing to do because it prevents you from throwing the words away, and increases your focus of gratitude. Saying *thank you* three times is also a magic formula, because it is the mathematical number of all new creation in the Universe. For example, it takes one male and one female to create a baby. The male, female, and baby total three, completing a new creation. The same rule of three applies to the creation of everything in the Universe, including the creation of your desires, and so when you say *thank you* three times in a row, you are using the magic number of creation, and a secret magic formula!

The second step of Make All Your Wishes Come True involves saturating your desires with even more gratitude. You can complete the second step at any time during the day today, either at the same time as listing your top ten desires, or intermittently throughout the day.

To saturate each of your desires with gratitude's magical power, begin with the first desire on your list and using your imagination mentally answer the following questions, as though you've received your desire:

1. What emotions did you feel when you received your desire?

2. Who was the first person you told when you received your desire, and how did you tell them?

3. What is the first great thing you did when you
    received your desire? Include as much detail as you
    can in your mind.

Finally, reread each desire, and really emphasize the
magic words, *thank you,* so that you feel them as much
as you can.

Move on to the second desire on your list, and
follow the same steps with each desire, until you've
completed all ten desires. Spend at least one minute on
each desire.

If you want to do something that's really powerful and
a lot of fun, you can also create a Magic Board, where
you attach pictures of your desires. Cut out the pictures
and attach them to a board that's in a place where you
will see it often. Place the magic words **THANK YOU,
THANK YOU, THANK YOU** in big bold letters on
your Magic Board. Or you can use your refrigerator as
your Magic Board. If you have a family, you can create
a Magic Board as a family project, because children
love it! Imagine that your Magic Board is truly magical,
and that whatever you place a picture of on your board
is instantly being moved toward you. Your continued
gratitude for it will magnetize it all the way into
your life.

MAGIC PRACTICE NUMBER 13

Make All Your Wishes Come True

1. Count Your Blessings: Make a list of ten blessings. Write *why* you're grateful. Reread your list, and at the end of each blessing say *thank you, thank you, thank you,* and feel as grateful for that blessing as you can.

2. Sit down at a computer or with a pen and journal, and list your top **ten** desires. Write *thank you* three times before each one, *as though you've already received it.* For example: *Thank you, thank you, thank you for _____your desire_____* .

3. Using your imagination, answer the following questions in your mind, as though you've received each of your ten desires:

   1. What emotions did you feel when you received your desire?

   2. Who was the first person you told when you received your desire, and how did you tell them?

   3. What is the first great thing you did when you received your desire? Include as much detail as you can in your mind.

4. Finally, reread the sentence listing your desire, and really emphasize the magic words, *thank you,* so that you feel them as much as you can.

5. If you like, create a Magic Board. Cut out pictures
    and attach them to your Magic Board, and put it in
    a place you see often. Title the board with **THANK
    YOU, THANK YOU, THANK YOU** in big bold
    letters across the top.

6. Just before you go to sleep tonight, hold your Magic
    Rock in one hand, and say the magic words, *thank
    you,* for the *best* thing that happened during the day.

Day 14

HAVE A MAGICAL DAY

*"Intentions compressed into words enfold
magical power."*

DEEPAK CHOPRA (B. 1946)
MEDICAL DOCTOR AND WRITER

To see and experience the most magical day of
your life, you can be grateful for your whole day *before*
you live it! To Have A Magical Day, you simply think
through your plans for the day and say the magic words,
thank you, for each one going well, *before* you've lived it.
It's the easiest thing to do, it only takes a few minutes,
but the difference it can make in your day is incredible.
Being grateful for your day beforehand creates a
magical day through the law of attraction; when you *give*
thanks for the experiences in your day going well, you
must *receive* back experiences going well!

If you don't believe you have the power to affect the
circumstances of your day so dramatically, think about
a time when you woke up grumpy or in a bad mood.

You went off into your day, and one thing after another went wrong, until by the end of the day you were exclaiming that you had a heck of a bad day – as though the bad day happened by accident. Well, the only reason you had a bad day was because you took your bad mood from the morning with you, and it was your bad mood that was the cause of one thing after another going wrong.

Even waking up in a bad mood doesn't happen by accident, because it means that you went to sleep thinking negatively about something, perhaps without realizing it. It's the very reason why you are doing the Magic Rock practice last thing at night, to ensure that you go to sleep thinking good thoughts. The Magic Rock practice at night combined with Count Your Blessings every morning sets your good mood at night and in the morning, and they guarantee that you are feeling good *before* you go off into your day.

To Have A Magical Day you need to feel good. I don't know of anything other than gratitude that guarantees to put you in a good mood almost instantly.

Whatever your plans are for the day today, whether it's traveling, a meeting, work project, lunch, exercise, dropping off dry cleaning, playing a sport, going to the theater, meeting a friend, yoga, cleaning your house, going to school, or buying groceries, turn today into a magical day by saying the magic words, *thank you,* for each plan going well – *before* you live it! If you're a person who writes daily lists of things you need to do, then you can go through your daily list and be grateful for each one having gone well. Whether you do this magical practice in your mind or on paper, the most important thing is that you feel the result of each plan or activity was the *best* it could have been.

When you use gratitude ahead of time to Have A Magical Day it wipes out unexpected problems or difficulties before they happen. The more you use this magical practice, the better your days will become, and from the smallest things to the important things, everything starts going well in your life. The bumpy days smooth out, and instead of frustrating or troublesome things happening in your day, your days start to have a magical flow about them, and things seem to magically go your way, with less effort, no worry, no stress, and far more joy.

When I first began to use gratitude to Have A Magical Day, I chose to give thanks ahead of time for the events in my day that I didn't enjoy doing very much. One of those things was going to the supermarket. At the beginning of the day I said the magic words: "Thank you for the easy and joyful trip to the supermarket." I had no idea how a trip to the supermarket could be easy and joyful, but I felt as much gratitude for that outcome as I could.

The result of gratitude's magical power was that I got a parking space right at the door. I then ran into two friends. One friend I hadn't seen for a long time, and we got together for lunch after shopping. The second friend I ran into told me about an amazing and inexpensive house cleaner, which was something I had been dreaming of having. As I did my supermarket shopping, wherever I looked, what I needed was magically in front of my eyes; everything was in stock on the shelves; one item after another was on special; and as I approached the checkout after doing my shopping in record time, a new aisle opened, and the checkout person signaled me to them. As the checkout person was putting my items through the register, out of the blue she asked, "Do you need any batteries?" It was the one item I had forgotten to buy! My trip to the supermarket was beyond easy and joyful – it was downright magical!

It only takes a few minutes in the morning to use gratitude to Have A Magical Day by giving thanks for the events in your day ahead of time, but this one practice alone will change the way your entire day unfolds.

To Have A Magical Day, when you wake up to the new day, either before you get out of bed, or while you're showering or getting dressed, think about your plans for the day, and give thanks for each one going brilliantly well. Make sure you do this magical practice at the beginning of your day and in one session. In your mind, work your way through the plans you have for the morning, afternoon, and evening, until bedtime. With each plan or event, say the magic words and imagine that you're saying *thank you* at the end of the day, and you're immensely grateful because it did go brilliantly well.

You can use as many superlatives as you like to help you feel more grateful. "*Thank you* for the incredibly successful meeting." "*Thank you* for the amazing outcome with the phone call." "*Thank you* for one of the best days ever at work." "*Thank you* for the thrilling sports game." "*Thank you* for the effortless and fun day of cleaning." "*Thank you* for the great night out with our friends." "*Thank you* for the relaxing day of travel." "*Thank you* for the amazing energy from my exercise session." "*Thank you* for the best family get-together we've ever had."

This magical practice is more powerful if you can say the magic words, *thank you,* out loud for each experience, but if you're not in a position to say them out loud then it is fine to say them in your mind.

After you've finished using gratitude's magical power for every task and event in your day, end the practice by saying, "And thank you for the great news coming to me today!" Without fail, every single morning when I finish using gratitude to Have A Magical Day, I give thanks for the great news coming to me that day. As a result, I've never received so much great news in my entire life. One week after another, one day after another, great news pours in! Each time I receive another piece of great news I am especially grateful and excited because I know I used gratitude's magical power to bring it, and then even more great news continues to come in. If you want to receive more great news than you ever have before, then just follow in my footsteps.

MAGIC PRACTICE NUMBER 14

Have a Magical Day

1. Count Your Blessings: Make a list of ten blessings. Write *why* you're grateful. Reread your list, and at the end of each blessing say *thank you, thank you, thank you,* and feel as grateful for that blessing as you can.

2. In the morning, work your way in your mind through the plans you have for the day and evening, until bedtime. With each plan or event, say the magic words, *thank you,* for it having gone well. Imagine that you're saying *thank you* at the end of the day, and you're immensely grateful because it went perfectly.

3. After you've finished being grateful for all the plans in your day going brilliantly well, end this magical practice by saying: *And thank you for the great news coming to me today!*

4. Just before you go to sleep tonight, hold your Magic Rock in one hand, and say the magic words, *thank you,* for the *best* thing that happened during the day.

Day 15
MAGICALLY HEAL YOUR RELATIONSHIPS

If you have a difficult or broken relationship, are suffering from a broken heart, or hold any resentment or blame toward another person for anything, you can change it through gratitude. Gratitude will magically improve any difficult relationship, whether that person is a husband or wife, brother or sister, son or daughter, partner, boss, business client, work colleague, mother- or father-in-law, parent, friend, or neighbor.

When we are faced with a difficult relationship or a challenging situation in a relationship, in almost all cases, we're not in the least bit grateful for the other person. Instead, we're busy blaming the other person for the problems we have with them, and that means we don't have a shred of gratitude. Blame is never going to make a relationship better, and it's never going to make your life better. In fact, the more you blame, the worse the relationship gets, and the worse your life gets.

Whether it's a current relationship or a past relationship, if you harbor bad feelings toward another person, practicing gratitude will eliminate those feelings. Why would you want to remove your bad feelings about another person?

> *"Holding on to anger is like grasping a hot coal with the intent of throwing it at someone else; you are the one who gets burned."*
>
> GAUTAMA BUDDHA (CIRCA 563 BC–483 BC)
> FOUNDER OF BUDDHISM

Bad feelings about another person burn *your* life, but gratitude will eliminate them!

For example, if you have an ex-partner who is connected to you through your children, and the relationship isn't good, look at your children's faces and realize that they wouldn't be alive if it wasn't for your ex-partner. Your children's lives are one of the most precious gifts you have. Look at your children, and give thanks to your ex-partner for their lives every single day! As well as bringing peace and harmony to the relationship, through your example you will be teaching your children the greatest tool for their life – gratitude.

Or, if you're suffering from a broken heart or grief due to a relationship having ended, you can use gratitude's magical power to transform your pain. Gratitude magically transforms emotional pain into healing and happiness faster than anything else, and the story of my parents is a perfect example of that.

My mother and father fell in love with each other
virtually at first sight. From the moment they met, they
were truly grateful to be with each other, and they had
the most beautiful marriage I have ever seen.

When my father died, my mother understandably
suffered from enormous grief. After months of
suffering, she began to use gratitude's magical power,
and despite her immense grief and pain, she looked for
things to be grateful for. She began with the past, and
she recalled all the wonderful times of happiness she
had received through the decades with my father. Then
she took the next big step, and she looked for things
to be grateful for in the future. One by one she found
them. She found or remembered things she had always
wanted to do but didn't have time to do when my father
was alive. And with this courageous step of gratitude,
opportunities to fulfill her dreams magically poured
in, and her life became rich with happiness again. The
magical power of gratitude gave my mother a new life.

For today's magical practice you are going to look for
a hot coal that is burning your life, and literally turn
it into gold through gratitude! Choose one difficult,
problematic, or broken relationship that you want
to improve. It doesn't matter whether the person is
currently in your life, or if it's a past relationship and
the person is no longer in your life.

Sit down and make a written list of ten things you're
grateful for about the person you've chosen. Think
back through the history of the relationship, and list
the great things about the person or the great things

you received from the relationship. The easiest way to do this is to think back to the way things were *before* the relationship deteriorated or ended. If the relationship was never good, then think hard about any good qualities in the person because they are there.

This magical practice is not about who is right or wrong. No matter what you feel someone has done to you, no matter what someone said or didn't do, *you* can magically heal the relationship, and you don't need the other person in order to heal it.

There is gold in every relationship, even the difficult ones, and to bring riches to all your relationships and your life, you have to find the gold. As you dig and discover a nugget of gold, write it down, address the person by name, and express your sentence in gratitude:

_____*Name*_____, *I'm grateful for* _____*what?*_____ .

1. *Paul, I'm grateful for our time together. While our marriage did end, I learned a lot, I am so much wiser today, and I use what I learned from our marriage in many of my relationships today.*

2. *Paul, I'm grateful for everything you did to try and make our marriage work, because ten years of marriage means you did try.*

3. *Paul, I am grateful to you for our children. The joy I receive from them every day could not be without you.*

4. *Paul, I'm grateful to you for the hard work and long hours you put in to support our family, while I was at home taking care of our children. It was a big responsibility to have all of us dependent on you, so thank you.*

5. *Paul, I am grateful to you for the precious moments I had with our children as they grew up. I got to see our children talk and walk for the first time, and I know you didn't have that opportunity.*

6. *Paul, I'm grateful for your support when I went through a difficult time of grief and loss.*

7. *Paul, I'm grateful to you for the times when I was sick, and you did your best to take care of me and the children.*

8. *Paul, I'm grateful for the great times we had, and we did have many.*

9. *Paul, I'm grateful that you want to continue to be a father to our children.*

10. *Paul, I'm grateful for your support and the time you want to give to our children. I know they mean as much to you as they do to me.*

By the time you've finished your gratitude list of ten things, you should feel much better about the person and the relationship. The ultimate point you want to reach is where you don't have any bad feelings toward the person anymore, because it's *your* life that is harmed by those feelings. Every relationship is different, and if need be, you may choose to repeat this magical practice over several days until you reach the point where you don't have any bad feelings toward the person anymore.

If you are using gratitude's magical power to improve a current relationship, you will see the relationship begin to change miraculously before your eyes. It only takes one person to magically change a relationship through gratitude, but it is the person who uses gratitude who receives the benefits in their whole life.

If you chose a past relationship, where you are not in contact with the person anymore, you will feel a peace and happiness fill you, and at the same time you will see other current relationships in your life magically improve.

In the future, if a relationship becomes challenging, remember to use this magical practice immediately. You will stop the difficulties before they get any bigger, and instead you will increase the magic in the relationship!

MAGIC PRACTICE NUMBER 15

Magically Heal Your Relationships

1. Count Your Blessings: Make a list of ten blessings. Write *why* you're grateful. Reread your list, and at the end of each blessing say *thank you, thank you, thank you,* and feel as grateful for that blessing as you can.

2. Choose **one** difficult, problematic, or broken relationship that you want to improve.

3. Sit down and make a written list of **ten** things you're grateful for about the person you've chosen. Write it down in the following way:

    _____*Name*_____ , I'm grateful for ____*what?*____ .

4. Just before you go to sleep tonight, hold your Magic Rock in one hand, and say the magic words, *thank you,* for the *best* thing that happened during the day.

Day 16
MAGIC AND MIRACLES IN HEALTH

"Miracles are not contrary to nature, but only contrary to what we know about nature."

SAINT AUGUSTINE (354–430)
THEOLOGIAN AND CATHOLIC BISHOP

We should feel healthy, energized, and full of happiness most of the time, because that is how it feels to have our birthright of full health. The reality, however, is that a lot of people don't feel this way very often, if ever. Many people are dealing with illnesses, problems with the functioning of their body, or suffering from bouts of depression and other mental health problems, which are all states of less-than-full health.

Gratitude is one of the fastest ways I know to magically begin experiencing the full state of health you are meant to have in your body and mind. All the miracles of healing we see happen are simply the result of full health being restored instantly in the human body, where before there was less than full and perfect health. If you don't think gratitude creates miracles in your health and body, then read some of the thousands of miracle stories on The Secret website: www.thesecret.tv/stories.

Gratitude's magical power *increases* the natural flow of health to the mind and body, and can assist the body in healing more quickly, as countless studies have shown. The magical power of gratitude also works hand in hand with good bodily care, nutrition, and any medical assistance you might have chosen to follow.

When there is some kind of sickness or condition in your body, it is understandable that you may have negative feelings about it, like worry, frustration, or fear. But having negative feelings about sickness does not restore health. In fact, it has the opposite effect – it reduces health even more. To increase your health, you need to replace the negative feelings with good feelings, and gratitude is the easiest way to do it.

Many people also have critical thoughts and feelings of dissatisfaction about their physical appearance. Unfortunately those thoughts and feelings also reduce the magical flow of health. When there's something you don't like about your body, you are not being grateful for your body. Think about it. By the law of attraction, complaints about your body bring more problems to complain about, and so complaining about your body or appearance puts your very health at risk.

*"Whoever does not have **gratitude** (for their health
and their body), even what he or she has will be taken
from him or her."*

*"Whoever has **gratitude** (for their health and their body)
will be given more, and he or she will have an abundance
(of health to their body)."*

You may be sick or unwell now, or even in a lot of pain,
but if you are reading these words you are continuing
to receive the gift of health. It can be very difficult to
access feelings of gratitude when sick or in pain, but
even the smallest bit of gratitude helps increase the
magical flow of health to the body.

Today's practice, Magic and Miracles in Health, is
designed to dramatically increase your health and
happiness. And we're going to take a triple-pronged
approach to accelerate the results.

Step 1: Health You've Received (past)

Think about the great health you have received
throughout your childhood, adolescence, and adult life.
Think about the times when you felt full of energy, and
you were happy. Recollect three separate times in your
mind when you felt on top of the world, say the magic
words, *thank you,* and feel sincere gratitude for those
times. If you think back to the big moments in your
life, you will be able to recollect three separate times
very easily.

Step 2: Health You're Continuing to Receive (present)

Think about the health you are continuing to receive today, and feel grateful for every organ, system, and physical sense that is currently working well in your body. Think about your arms, legs, hands, eyes, ears, liver, kidneys, brain, or heart. Choose five functions of your body that *are* well, and one by one, mentally say the magic words, *thank you,* for each one.

Step 3: Health You Want to Receive (future)

You're going to choose one thing you want to improve about your body for today's magical practice, but you are going to use gratitude's magical power for it in a very particular way. Think about the *ideal* state of what you want to improve. When you give thanks for the *ideal* state of anything, you have put into motion to receive back that ideal state.

Very often when a person is diagnosed with an illness or disease of some kind, they will not only talk about it a lot, but they will research the disease, gathering information about its possible worsening symptoms and dreaded outcomes. In other words, they give their entire focus to the disease. However, the law of attraction says that we can't make a problem go away by focusing on it, because focusing on the problem can only make the problem worse. Instead, we should do the exact opposite, and focus on the *ideal* state for the area of our body that is unwell, and give our thoughts and feelings to that. Gratitude for the *ideal* state of any part of our body powerfully uses our thoughts and feelings together so we magnetize it to us – in one fell swoop!

Spend one minute in visualizing a scene of yourself with the *ideal* state of your body that you want. And as you see your body in your mind the way you want it to be, be grateful for it as though you have received it.

So, if you want to magically restore health to your kidneys, be grateful for strong and healthy kidneys that filter and sift out all the waste products from your body. If you want to magically restore health to your blood, be grateful for pure and healthy blood that flows oxygen and nutrients to all parts of your body. If you want to magically restore health to your heart, give thanks for a strong and healthy heart that maintains the well-being of every organ in your body.

If you want to magically improve your eyesight, then give thanks for excellent vision. If you want to improve your hearing, then give thanks for perfect hearing. If you want more flexibility, then give thanks for a perfectly supple and agile body. If you want to change your weight, first think about the *ideal* weight that you want to be, then imagine yourself at that ideal weight, and give thanks for it as though you have received it now.

Whatever it is that you want to improve, first imagine yourself with the *ideal* state, and then be grateful for the *ideal* state as though you have received it right now.

> *"Natural forces within us are the true healers*
> *of disease."*
>
> HIPPOCRATES (CIRCA 460–CIRCA 370 BC)
> FATHER OF WESTERN MEDICINE

You can follow the Magic and Miracles in Health practice every day if you need to, and you can do it multiple times in a day if you really want to accelerate the magical restoration of full health, or the improvement of an aspect of your body. But it is vital that whenever you have a negative thought or feeling about the current state of your body or health that you replace it immediately by visualizing yourself with the *ideal* state you want and by being truly grateful, as though you have already received it.

The most effective way to guarantee health, other than taking good care of yourself physically, is to continue to be grateful for your health.

Magic Practice Number 16

Magic and Miracles in Health

1. Count Your Blessings: Make a list of ten blessings. Write *why* you're grateful. Reread your list, and at the end of each blessing say *thank you, thank you, thank you,* and feel as grateful for that blessing as you can.

2. Recollect **three** separate times throughout your life when you felt on top of the world, and give sincere thanks for those times.

3. Think about **five** functions of your body that *are* well, and one by one give thanks for each one.

4. Choose **one** thing about your body or health you want to improve, and spend one minute visualizing yourself with the *ideal* state of your body or health. Then give thanks for this *ideal* state.

5. Just before you go to sleep tonight, hold your Magic Rock in one hand, and say the magic words, *thank you,* for the *best* thing that happened during the day.

Day 17
THE MAGIC CHECK

*"In the magical universe there are no coincidences
and there are no accidents. Nothing happens unless
someone wills it to happen."*

WILLIAM S. BURROUGHS (1914–1997)
WRITER AND POET

When you direct gratitude's magical power toward
any negative condition, a *new* condition is created,
eliminating the old condition. That means that when
you get yourself to the place where you feel grateful
for money more than you feel a lack of money, a new
condition is created, eliminating the lack of money and
magically replacing it with more money.

All bad feelings about money push money away from
you and reduce the amount of money in your life, and
every time you feel bad about money you reduce it a
little more. If you have feelings about money like envy,
disappointment, worry, or fear, you cannot receive
more. The law of attraction says that like attracts

like, so if you feel disappointed that you don't have enough money, you will receive more disappointing circumstances of not having enough money. If you are worried about money you will receive more worrying situations about money. If you feel fearful about the state of your money, then you must receive more situations that will continue to make you fearful about money.

However difficult it may be, you have to ignore your current situation and any lack of money you may currently be experiencing, and gratitude is the guaranteed way for you to do that. You can't be grateful for money and disappointed about money at the same time. You can't be thinking grateful thoughts about money and have worried thoughts about money at the same time. Nor can you be grateful for money and have fearful thoughts about money at the same time. When you're grateful for money, not only do you stop the negative thoughts and feelings that push money away from you, you're doing the very thing that brings more money to you!

You have already practiced gratitude for the money you have received and continue to receive. So, before you use gratitude's magical power for the money you want, you need to understand the various ways and avenues that money or riches could come into your life. Because if you're not grateful each time your riches or money increase, you will stop the abundance from flowing to you.

Money can come to you through receiving an unexpected check, an increase in salary, a lottery win, a tax refund, or an unanticipated gift of money from someone. Your money can also increase when somebody else spontaneously picks up the tab for coffee, lunch, or dinner, when you're about to purchase an item and you discover it has been discounted, when there's a money-back offer on a purchase, or when someone gives you a gift of something you needed to buy. The end result of every one of these circumstances is that you have more money! So whenever a situation arises, ask yourself: does this circumstance mean that I have more money? Because if it does, you need to be very grateful for the money you're receiving through that circumstance!

If you tell a friend you're about to buy an item and the friend offers to lend or give you the very item because they don't use it, or if you're planning to travel and you hear about a discounted special that you end up taking, or if your lending institution lowers their interest rate, or a service provider offers you a far better package, your money magically increased through the saving of money. Are you getting the idea of the unlimited situations where you can receive money?

Most likely you've experienced some of these situations in the past, and whether you realized it or not at the time, they occurred because you attracted them. But when gratitude is your way of life, you attract magical situations all the time! Many people call it good luck, but it's not luck at all; it's Universal law.

Any circumstance that results in you having more money or receiving something that cost money is a result of *your* gratitude. You'll feel great joy in knowing that you did it, and when you combine your joy with your gratitude, you have a real magnetic force that will keep attracting more and more abundance.

When I arrived in the United States several years ago, I arrived with two suitcases. I worked in a bare-bones apartment with my computer on my lap. I didn't have a car, and so I mostly walked everywhere. But I was grateful for everything. I was grateful to be in the United States, I was grateful for the work I was doing, I was grateful for the bare-bones apartment with its four plates, four knives, four forks, and four spoons. I was grateful that I could walk to most places, and I was grateful that there was a taxi stand right across the street. Then something incredible happened – a person I knew decided to gift to me a driver and a car for a few months. Other than my computer, I was living with the most basic material things to survive, and then suddenly I had my own personal driver and car! I was grateful, so I was given more. And that is exactly how the magic happens with gratitude.

Today's magical practice for the money you want to receive has brought astounding results to many people. At the end of this practice you will find a blank Magic Check from the Gratitude Bank of the Universe, and you are going to write out the Magic Check to yourself. Fill in the amount of money you want to receive, along with your name and today's date. Choose a specific amount of money for one thing you *really* want, because you will be able to feel more gratitude for the money when you know what you're going to spend the money on. Money is a means to what you want, but it's not the end result, so if you just thought about money per se you wouldn't be able to feel as much gratitude. When you imagine getting the things you *really* want, or doing the things you *really* want to do, you will feel far more gratitude than if you were just being grateful for money.

You can photocopy or scan the Magic Check from the book. You can also get an abundance of blank Magic Checks from: www.thesecret.tv/magiccheck.

If you want you can start with a smaller amount on your first Magic Check, and after you receive the smaller amount, you can keep increasing the amounts on your next checks. The benefit of starting with a smaller amount is that when you magically receive it you will know that *you* did it, you will know absolutely that the magic of gratitude worked, and the gratitude and joy you feel will make bigger amounts believable to you.

Once you have filled in the details of the Magic Check, hold the check in your hands and think about the specific thing you want the money for. Get a picture in your mind and visualize yourself actually using the money to get the very thing that you want, and put as much excitement and gratitude into it as you can.

Maybe you want the money for a new pair of shoes, a computer, or a new bed, so picture yourself actually buying what you want in a store. If you would purchase

what you want online, then picture yourself receiving
the delivery, so you feel excitement and gratitude.
You might want the money to travel overseas, or for
your child's college education, so imagine buying your
airplane ticket, or opening a college bank account. And
feel as happy and grateful as if you've really received it!

After you've completed these steps, take the Magic
Check with you today, or put it in a place where you will
see it often. On at least two more occasions during the
day today take the Magic Check in your hands, picture
yourself actually using the money for what you wanted,
and feel as grateful and excited as you can, as though
you are really doing it. If you want you can do it more
times in the day. As with any other magical practice, you
can't do it too often.

At the end of today, either keep your Magic Check
where you had it, or put it in another prominent place
where you will see it daily. You could put it on your
bathroom mirror, your refrigerator, underneath your
Magic Rock, in your car or wallet, or on the background
of your computer. Any time you see your Magic Check,
feel as though you've received the money, and be
grateful that now you can have or do what you want.

When you have received the money on your Magic
Check, or if you receive the item you wanted to spend
the money on in another magical way, replace the check
with a new amount for something else that you *really*
want, and continue with the Magic Check practice as
long as you want.

MAGIC PRACTICE NUMBER 17

The Magic Check

1. Count Your Blessings: Make a list of ten blessings. Write *why* you're grateful. Reread your list, and at the end of each blessing say *thank you, thank you, thank you,* and feel as grateful for that blessing as you can.

2. Fill in your Magic Check with the amount of money you want to receive, along with your name and today's date.

3. Hold your Magic Check in your hands, and imagine purchasing the specific thing you want the money for. Feel as happy and grateful as you can that you have received it.

4. Take the Magic Check with you today, or put it in a place where you will see it often. On at least **two** more occasions, take the check in your hands, picture yourself using the money for what you want, and feel as grateful as though you were really doing it.

5. At the end of today, keep your Magic Check in a prominent place where you will see it daily. When you have received the money on your check, or if you receive the item you wanted to spend the money on, replace the check with a new amount for something else you want, and repeat steps 2–4.

6. Just before you go to sleep tonight, hold your Magic
    Rock in one hand, and say the magic words, *thank
    you*, for the *best* thing that happened during the day.

Photocopy or scan the check, then fill in the date, your name, and the amount you wish to receive in the currency of your choice.

THE GRATITUDE BANK OF THE UNIVERSE

DATE _____

the MAGIC CHECK

REMITTANCE ADVICE – Gratitude

PAY

TO THE ORDER OF

NOT NEGOTIABLE
You must believe
and be grateful to receive

the Universe

SIGNED:

DRAWER: THE GRATITUDE BANK OF THE UNIVERSE
ACCOUNT: UNLIMITED ABUNDANCE

This is not an instrument subject to Article 3 of the UCC

|: 843 62442 |: 843 732738 843

www.thesecret.tv

Day 18

THE MAGICAL TO-DO LIST

"The world is full of magical things waiting for our wits to grow sharper."

EDEN PHILLPOTTS (1862–1960)
NOVELIST AND POET

Really, when you think about it, gratitude is your best friend. It is always there for you, always available to help you, it will never fail you or let you down, and the more heavily you lean on it, the more it will do for you, and the more it will enrich your life. Today's magical practice will show you how to lean on gratitude even more, so it can do far more magical things *for* you.

Every day there are little life problems that come up and that need solving. Sometimes we can feel overwhelmed if we don't know how to solve a situation. Maybe your problem is that you don't have enough time for all the things you need to do, and you're at a loss because there are only twenty-four hours in the day. It may be that you feel overwhelmed from work,

and you want more free time, but you can't see any way
to have it. You may be at home taking care of children,
and you're feeling frazzled or exhausted, but you don't
have the means to get support to give you time out. You
may be faced with a problem that needs fixing, but you
have no idea which way to turn to fix it. You may have
lost something and tried your best to locate it, but had
no luck. Or you might want to find something, like
the perfect pet, perfect babysitter, great hairdresser,
or amazing dentist or doctor, and despite your best
efforts, you haven't been able to find what you need.
You could be in an uncomfortable situation because of
something a person has asked you to do, and you don't
know how to respond to them. Or you could be in some
kind of dispute with someone, and instead of getting it
resolved, things seem to be getting worse.

This Magical To-Do List practice will help you with any
little day-to-day problems when you don't know what to
do, or when you simply want something to be done for
you. You will be amazed at the results!

When you combine gratitude's magical power with the
law of attraction, people, circumstances, and events
must be rearranged to do what you want done *for* you!
You will not know how it will happen, or how it will be
done for you, and that is not your job. Your job is simply
to be as grateful as you can be for what you want done
right now, as though it were done. And then let the
magic happen!

Today, create a written to-do list of the most important
things you would like to be done or resolved *for* you,

and title your list The Magical To-Do List. You might put things on your list that you don't have time to do, or don't want to do, along with any current problems, from the smallest day-to-day things to bigger life situations. Think through any area of your life where you need something resolved or done for you.

When you've finished making your list, choose three things from your list to focus on today, and one at a time imagine that each item has been magically done *for* you. Imagine that all people, circumstances, and events have been moved to do it for you, and it is now done! All done, all sorted, all solved for you, and you are giving massive thanks in return for it having been done. Spend at least one minute on each of your three items, believing it is done, and feeling enormous gratitude in return. You can follow the same practice on the rest of the items on your list at another time, but there is power in simply putting the things you want done on the Magical To-Do List.

Remember that the law of attraction says "like attracts like," and that means that when you are grateful for the solutions as though you have them, you will attract everything you need into your life to resolve the situation. Focusing on problems attracts more problems. You have to be a magnet to the solution, not a magnet to the problem. Being grateful that you have the solution, and that it has been resolved, attracts the solution.

To demonstrate how powerful this magical practice is I want to share a story with you about my daughter, who used this practice to attract her lost wallet back to her.

After being out one night, my daughter discovered the next morning that she did not have her wallet, and she had no idea where she might have lost it, or even if it had been stolen. She called the restaurant where she went to dinner, the taxi company she used to come home, the local police station, and she searched the streets and knocked on surrounding doors. But no one had found her wallet.

Other than the fact that my daughter's wallet contained the usual precious things in it, including all her bank and credit cards, driver's license, and cash, her biggest concern was that her wallet contained no current contact information, because she had been overseas for some time. She didn't have a publicly listed phone number, and with a common surname, there seemed to be no hope.

But despite the seemingly impossible obstacles, my daughter sat down, closed her eyes, and got a picture of her wallet in her mind. She visualized that she was holding her wallet in her hands; she opened her wallet, she went through all its contents, and she felt enormous gratitude that she had her wallet and everything in it back and in her hands.

For the rest of the day, whenever she thought of it, again my daughter imagined she had her wallet in her hands, and she felt enormous elation and gratitude that her wallet had been returned to her.

Later that night she received a call from a farmer who lived one hundred miles away, saying that he had found her wallet. The extraordinary part of this story is that the farmer had found the wallet in the street outside my daughter's home in the early hours of the morning, and he immediately searched the wallet looking for contact details. He made several calls in trying to find its owner, but to no avail, and so he gave up, and drove back to his farm with the wallet.

But while he was walking out in the fields at his farm, the wallet kept nagging and nagging at him, and he decided to search through it one last time. He found a small piece of paper with a man's Christian name written on it, and so he put the Christian name together with my daughter's surname, and called directory assistance. There was just one listing for that Christian name and surname. The farmer called the phone number, and it was the home of my daughter's father. To this day we do not know how the farmer got that phone number, because it was an unlisted number! We called directory assistance ourselves several times after this happened, and the response every time was: "Sorry, there is no listing for that name."

From one hundred miles away, through the most extraordinary sequence of seemingly impossible events, my daughter's wallet was returned to her intact. She fulfilled her part in being grateful that she had her wallet back, and as must happen, gratitude performed its magic and moved every person, circumstance, and event to return her wallet to her.

The magical power of gratitude is available for you to use as well, and it always has been – you just had to discover it for yourself, and learn how to use it!

Magic Practice Number 18

The Magical To-Do List

1.   Count Your Blessings: Make a list of ten blessings.
     Write *why* you're grateful. Reread your list, and at
     the end of each blessing say *thank you, thank you,
     thank you,* and feel as grateful for that blessing as
     you can.

2.   Create a written list of the most important things or
     problems you need done or solved. Title your list
     The Magical To-Do List.

3.   Choose **three** of the most important things from
     your list, and one at a time, imagine that each thing
     has been done *for* you.

4.   Spend at least **one** minute on each thing, believing
     it is done, and feeling enormous gratitude in return.

5.   Just before you go to sleep tonight, hold your Magic
     Rock in one hand, and say the magic words, *thank
     you,* for the *best* thing that happened during the day.

Day 19
MAGIC FOOTSTEPS

*"A hundred times every day I remind myself that my
inner and outer life depend on the labors of other men,
living and dead, and that I must exert myself in order
to give in the same measure as I have received and am
still receiving."*

ALBERT EINSTEIN (1879–1955)
NOBEL PRIZE–WINNING PHYSICIST

With those words, Einstein gave us a gift equal to
his scientific discoveries. He gave us one of the magical
secrets to his success. Gratitude – every day!

Einstein is the inspiration behind today's magical
practice, and you are going to follow in his footsteps to
bring success to *your* life. Today, like Einstein, you will
say *thank you* one hundred times, and you're going to
do it by taking one hundred Magic Footsteps. While it
might seem unbelievable to you that taking footsteps
can make a difference to your life, you will discover that
it is one of the most powerful things you can do.

*"God gave you a gift of 86,400 seconds today.
Have you used one to say 'thank you'?"*

WILLIAM A. WARD (1921–1994)
WRITER

To take Magic Footsteps, you take one step and in
your mind say the magic words, *thank you,* as your foot
touches the ground, and then again say *thank you* as
your other foot touches the ground. One foot, *thank
you,* next foot, *thank you,* and continue saying the magic
words with every footstep.

The best thing about Magic Footsteps is that you can
take any number of Magic Footsteps anywhere and
at any time; through your house from one room to
another, walking to get your lunch or coffee, taking the
trash out, walking to a business meeting, on your way to
catch a cab, train, or bus. You can take Magic Footsteps
on your way to anything that is important to you, like
exams, a date, a job interview, an audition, to meet a
client, to the bank, ATM, dentist, doctor, hairdresser,
to see your team play in a sports game, down corridors,
through airport terminals, in parks, or from one block
to another.

I take Magic Footsteps around my home, from my
bed to my bathroom, kitchen to my bedroom, and
outside to my car and the mailbox. Whenever I walk
down a street, or walk anywhere, I choose a point as
my destination, and I put gratitude in my footsteps
all the way.

If you take notice of how you're feeling before you begin, then you will notice a big difference in how you feel after you've taken Magic Footsteps. It doesn't matter if you can't get much of a feeling of gratitude while you're taking them; I promise you will still feel happier afterward. If you're feeling down, Magic Footsteps will make you feel better, and even if you're feeling great, Magic Footsteps will lift your spirits even higher!

To take the most effective Magic Footsteps, take Magic Footsteps for about ninety seconds; this is how long it will take the average person to take one hundred steps at a leisurely pace. This practice is not about taking one hundred steps exactly, but taking at least that number of steps, because it will probably take that number of footsteps to make a difference to the way you feel. Once you're clear on the approximate distance you can take your one hundred steps of gratitude any time during the day. Don't count the footsteps when you're doing the practice, because you'll be counting instead of saying *thank you,* the magic words, with each step.

When you have completed today's magical practice you will have said the magic words, *thank you,* one hundred times! How many days of your life have you said *thank you* one hundred times?

And Einstein did it every day!

Magic Practice Number 19

Magic Footsteps

1. Count Your Blessings: Make a list of ten blessings. Write *why* you're grateful. Reread your list, and at the end of each blessing say *thank you, thank you, thank you,* and feel as grateful for that blessing as you can.

2. Take **one hundred** Magic Footsteps (for about ninety seconds) in gratitude any time during the day.

3. With each footstep, say and feel the magic words, *thank you.*

4. Just before you go to sleep tonight, hold your Magic Rock in one hand, and say the magic words, *thank you,* for the *best* thing that happened during the day.

Day 20
HEART MAGIC

"Gratitude is the memory of the heart."

JEAN-BAPTISTE MASSIEU (1743–1818)
FRENCH REVOLUTION ACTIVIST

You might have figured out by now that with any magical practice of gratitude the aim is always to feel it as much as you can. This is because when you increase the feeling of gratitude on the inside, the things you have to be grateful for in the outside world increase too.

Eventually, after practicing gratitude for a long period of time, you will automatically feel it deeply in your heart. However, today's magical practice will collapse the time it would normally take for you to reach that level.

The Heart Magic practice is designed to powerfully increase the depths that you feel gratitude, by focusing your mind on the area of your heart as you say and feel the magic words, *thank you*. Scientific research has shown that by focusing on your heart as you feel gratitude, the rhythm of your heart immediately becomes much more even and harmonious, resulting in major improvements to your immune system and health. That gives you an idea of the power of Heart Magic. It takes a little practice the first time you try it, but it is worth the effort. After a few times you will get it, and each time you practice it your feeling of gratitude will increase exponentially.

To practice Heart Magic, focus your mind and your attention on the area around your heart. It doesn't matter if you focus on the inside or the outside of your body. Close your eyes, because it will make it easier, and while keeping your mind focused on your heart, mentally say the magic words, *thank you*. Once you've practiced it a few times, you won't need to close your eyes anymore, but as a general rule, you will feel more gratitude when you close your eyes.

There are several things you can do to help you get Heart Magic down really quickly. You can put your right hand on the area around your heart to keep your mind focused there while you say the magic words, *thank you*. Or you can imagine that the magic words, *thank you,* are coming out of your heart rather than your mind as you say them.

As part of today's magical practice, take your Top Ten Desire List and practice Heart Magic on each desire. Read each desire in your mind or out loud, and when you get to the end of reading each one, close your eyes, focus your mind on the area around your heart, keep your mind on your heart area, and say the magic words again, *thank you,* slowly. Again, you can use the tips I've given above if it helps you. After you have finished Heart Magic on each of your desires, you will have not only increased the depth of gratitude you are able to reach, you will also have dramatically increased your gratitude for your top desires.

You can continue to practice Heart Magic on your desires regularly if you want to speed up the receiving of them, or you can use Heart Magic any time you say the magic words, *thank you.* Even just using Heart Magic a couple of times a day will have a big effect on your happiness and on the magic in your life.

Once you have practiced Heart Magic a few times you will feel a huge increase in the depth of your feeling, and with gratitude it's all about the depth of the feeling, because the deeper the feeling the greater the abundance you will receive. The initial physical signs that you've increased the depth of your feeling could be that you get a tingling feeling around your heart, or feel a wave of joy rush through your body. Your eyes may fill with tears, or you may get goose bumps. But without exception, you will begin to feel a depth of peace and happiness you've never felt before!

MAGIC PRACTICE NUMBER 20

Heart Magic

1. Count Your Blessings: Make a list of ten blessings. Write *why* you're grateful. Reread your list, and at the end of each blessing say *thank you, thank you, thank you,* and feel as grateful for that blessing as you can.

2. Focus your mind and your attention on the area around your heart.

3. Close your eyes, and while keeping your mind focused on your heart, mentally say the magic words, *thank you.*

4. Take your Top Ten Desire List and practice Heart Magic by reading each desire, then closing your eyes, focusing your mind on the area around your heart, and slowly saying *thank you,* again.

5. Just before you go to sleep tonight, hold your Magic Rock in one hand, and say the magic words, *thank you,* for the *best* thing that happened during the day.

Day 21
MAGNIFICENT OUTCOMES

> *"You say grace before meals. All right. But I say grace before the concert and the opera, and grace before the play and pantomime, and grace before I open a book, and grace before sketching, painting, swimming, fencing, boxing, walking, playing, dancing and grace before I dip the pen in the ink."*

G. K. CHESTERTON (1874–1936)
WRITER

We all want good outcomes to everything we do. In giving thanks *before* he performed an action, the writer Gilbert Keith Chesterton used the magic of gratitude to guarantee the outcome he wanted.

You will have had times when you thought to yourself, "I hope this goes well," or, "I hope this turns out okay," or, "I'm going to need a lot of luck." All these thoughts are *hoping* for a good outcome to a situation. But life doesn't happen by chance or because of a stroke of luck. The laws of the Universe operate mathematically to the finest possible degree; that is something you can count on!

A pilot doesn't *hope* that the laws of physics will keep working during his flight, because he knows the laws of physics will never fail. You don't go into your day and *hope* that the law of gravity will keep you on the ground so you don't float off into space. You know there's no chance at play, and gravity's law will never fail.

If you want Magnificent Outcomes to everything you do, then you have to use the law that governs outcomes – the law of attraction. That means you have to use your thoughts and feelings to *attract* Magnificent Outcomes to you, and being grateful for Magnificent Outcomes is one of the simplest ways to do it.

The Magnificent Outcomes practice is being grateful *before* you do something you want to go well. You could be grateful for the magnificent outcome to the work meeting, job interview, or exam, the magnificent outcome to the sports game, phone call, catch-up with a friend, or seeing your mother-in-law. You could be grateful for the magnificent outcome to your exercise routine, your pet's vet appointment, or your medical or dental checkup. You could be grateful for the magnificent outcome when an electrician, plumber, or any tradesperson is addressing a problem in your home, the magnificent outcome to a family outing, conversation with your child about their behavior, or heart to heart with your partner. You could be grateful for the magnificent outcome to a purchase you will be making, such as a birthday gift, engagement ring, or wedding dress, or the magnificent outcome to choosing a new cell phone, new carpet, drapes, or renovation company. You could be grateful for the magnificent outcome for a reservation at a restaurant, or great seats for a concert, the magnificent outcome to your daily mail, your daily emails, or your tax refund for the year.

If it helps you to believe in the magical power of gratitude to create Magnificent Outcomes, you can wave your fingers through the air and imagine you're sprinkling magic dust over the event you want to turn out magnificently!

Another time to use gratitude for Magnificent Outcomes is when something unexpected happens during your day. When something unexpected happens, very often we can jump to conclusions and immediately think there's something wrong. For example, you arrive at work and are told that the boss wants to see you right away. The problem with jumping to conclusions and thinking there's something wrong is that the law of attraction says that what you think and feel you will attract to you. So instead of jumping to conclusions and thinking you might be in trouble, take the opportunity to make the magic happen by being grateful for a magnificent outcome.

If you miss your bus or train on your way to work, or miss a flight, or are unexpectedly delayed, instead of thinking, "This is bad," be grateful for the magnificent outcome so that you put the magic into motion to *receive* a magnificent outcome.

If you're a parent and you're asked to attend an unexpected meeting at school about your child, instead of thinking there's a problem, be grateful for the magnificent outcome. If you receive an unexpected phone call, email, or letter, and the thought flashes into your mind, "I wonder what's wrong," immediately be grateful for the magnificent outcome, *before* you pick up the call, or open the email or letter.

Most of the time you will see and experience the magnificent outcome you asked for, and occasionally you won't even know how you benefited from an unexpected event. But when you ask for a magnificent outcome and feel sincerely grateful for it, you are using the mathematical law of attraction, and you must receive a magnificent outcome back, somewhere, at some time. Guaranteed!

Whenever you find yourself thinking there's chance at play with something in your life, or thinking you have no control over something, or when you find yourself *hoping* something will turn out well, remember that there's no chance for the law of attraction – you will get what you're thinking and feeling. Gratitude helps protect you from attracting what you don't want – bad outcomes – and it ensures you get what you do want – Magnificent Outcomes!

When you are grateful for Magnificent Outcomes, you are using Universal law, and changing hopes and chance into faith and certainty. When gratitude becomes your way of life, you automatically go into everything you do with gratitude, *knowing* that the magic of gratitude will produce a magnificent outcome.

The more you practice Magnificent Outcomes, and make it a daily habit, the more Magnificent Outcomes you will attract into your life. Less and less you will find yourself in situations that you don't want to be in. You won't find yourself in the wrong place at the wrong time. And no matter what happens in your day, you will know with absolute certainty that the outcome will be magnificent.

At the beginning of today, choose three separate situations where you would like Magnificent Outcomes. You can choose three things that are important to you in your life currently, such as a job interview coming up, an application for a loan, an exam, or a doctor's appointment. You can also start by selecting three things that are normally humdrum activities for you, because when the magic happens to those humdrum activities you will be really convinced that you attracted the magnificent outcome! For example, you could choose your drive to work, doing the ironing, going to the bank or post office, picking up the kids, paying the bills, or collecting the mail.

Make a written list of the three situations you've chosen for Magnificent Outcomes. Use gratitude's magical power, and as you write each one imagine that you're writing about each one *after* it has happened:

Thank you for the magnificent outcome to _____!

For the second step of this magical practice, you are going to choose three unexpected things that arise today and use the magical power of gratitude for their Magnificent Outcomes as well. You could do this practice before you take three phone calls, or before you open three emails or three letters in the mail, before you do an unexpected errand, or anything else unexpected that comes up in the day. This part of the practice is not so much about what unexpected events you choose as it is about you practicing gratitude for Magnificent Outcomes on the little unexpected things. Each time an unexpected event arises, close your eyes briefly if you can, and mentally say and feel the magic words:

Thank you for the magnificent outcome to _____!

You can't do this magical practice too much, because the more you practice it, the more Magnificent Outcomes you will have in your life as a matter of course. But practicing it today will get you into the idea of it, and in the future, if you ever find yourself in a situation where you're *hoping* for a good outcome or thinking you need luck, you will immediately turn to the magical power of gratitude, and make Magnificent Outcomes a certainty in your life!

MAGIC PRACTICE NUMBER 21

Magnificent Outcomes

1. Count Your Blessings: Make a list of ten blessings. Write *why* you're grateful. Reread your list, and at the end of each blessing say *thank you, thank you, thank you,* and feel as grateful for that blessing as you can.

2. At the beginning of the day, choose **three** things or situations that are important to you where you want Magnificent Outcomes.

3. List your three things, and write each one as though you are writing after it has happened: *Thank you for the magnificent outcome to _____!*

4. As you go through your day, choose **three** unexpected events that come up in your day where you can be grateful for a magnificent outcome. Each time, close your eyes and mentally say and feel: *Thank you for the magnificent outcome to _____!*

5. Just before you go to sleep tonight, hold your Magic Rock in one hand, and say the magic words, *thank you,* for the *best* thing that happened during the day.

Day 22
BEFORE YOUR VERY EYES

"This world, after all our science and sciences, is still a miracle; wonderful, inscrutable, magical, and more to whosoever will think of it."

THOMAS CARLYLE (1795–1881)
WRITER AND HISTORIAN

Seven years ago, when I first discovered The Secret and the magical power of gratitude, I made a list of all of my desires. It was a long list! At that time, there seemed to be no possible way my desires could come true. Nevertheless, I took my top ten desires and I carried them with me on a piece of paper every day. Whenever I had an opportunity, I would take out my list and read through it, giving as much gratitude for each desire as I could, as though I had received it. With my number one desire, the desire I wanted more than anything else, I kept it constantly in my mind, and I would say the magic words, *thank you,* for it multiple times in a day, and feel as if it had come true. One by one every desire on my list magically appeared before my very eyes. As I received my desires I would cross them off my list, and when I had new desires I would add them to my list.

One of my desires from my original long list was to travel to Bora Bora near Tahiti. After spending a beautiful week at the exact place in Bora Bora I had listed, another beautiful thing happened. I was flying to the mainland of Tahiti on my way home when the airplane stopped en route to pick up passengers. The flight had been empty, but it filled to the brim with native Tahitians, and suddenly laughter, smiling faces, and a happiness that was palpable surrounded me.

As I enjoyed the short flight with these beautiful people, it became crystal clear to me the reason why they were so happy. They were grateful! They were grateful to be alive, they were grateful to be on the airplane, they were grateful to be with each other, they were grateful for where they were going – they were grateful for everything! I could have stayed on that plane and traveled around the world with them, it felt so good to be with them. And then it struck me that I had just received my final desire; Bora Bora was the last desire on my original long list, and the reason I was on that plane was before my very eyes – gratitude!

I've shared this story as an inspiration for you, because no matter how big your desires seem to be, you *can* receive them through gratitude. Even more than that, gratitude will bring a joy and happiness for life that you've never felt before, and that is truly priceless.

From the time I began using gratitude and the law
of attraction to the time I received my final desire on
my original list was four years. To give you an idea of
the enormousness of receiving all my desires in that
amount of time, when I created my desire list, my
company was two million dollars in debt, and I had
two months before I would be forced to shut it down
and would lose my home and everything I owned. The
money I owed on my personal credit cards was a small
fortune, and yet on my desire list was to own a big
house overlooking the ocean, to travel to exotic places
in the world, to have paid all my debts, to expand my
company, to restore every relationship to the best it
could be, improve the quality of my family's lives, to be
one hundred percent healthy again, and have unlimited
energy and excitement for life, along with the usual
list of material things. And my number one desire,
which seemed like an absolute impossibility to many of
the people around me, was to bring joy to millions of
people through my work.

The very *first* desire that I received was bringing joy
to millions of people through my work. The rest of
my desires magically followed, and one by one, as
they appeared before my very eyes, I crossed them
off my list.

So now it's your turn to use gratitude's magical power
to make your desires appear before your very eyes. At
the start of the day, take your Top Ten Desire List that
you created. Read through each sentence and desire on
your list, and for one minute imagine or visualize that

you have received your desire. Feel as much gratitude as you can, as if you have it now.

Carry your desire list with you today in your pocket. On at least two occasions in the day, take out your list, read through it, and feel as much gratitude for each one as you can, as though you've received it.

If you want your desires to come more quickly, I would highly recommend that you carry your desire list with you in your wallet or purse from this day forward, and whenever you have time, open it up, read through it, and feel as much gratitude as you can for each one. When your desires appear before your very eyes, cross them off your list, and add more. And if you're like me, each time you cross a desire off your list you will be in tears of joy, because what seemed impossible was made possible through the magical power of gratitude.

Magic Practice Number 22

Before Your Very Eyes

1. Count Your Blessings: Make a list of ten blessings. Write *why* you're grateful. Reread your list, and at the end of each blessing say *thank you, thank you, thank you,* and feel as grateful for that blessing as you can.

2. At the start of the day, take your Top Ten Desire List that you created.

3. Read through each sentence and desire on your list, and and for one minute imagine or visualize that you have received your desire. Feel as much gratitude as you can.

4. Carry your desire list with you today in your pocket. On at least **two** occasions in the day, take out your list, read through it, and feel as much gratitude as you can.

5. Just before you go to sleep tonight, hold your Magic Rock in one hand, and say the magic words, *thank you,* for the *best* thing that happened during the day.

Day 23

THE MAGICAL AIR
THAT YOU BREATHE

*"It is quite possible to leave your home for a walk
in the early morning air and return a different
person – beguiled, enchanted."*

MARY ELLEN CHASE (1887–1973)
EDUCATOR AND WRITER

If someone had told me a few years back to be
grateful for the air that I breathe, I would have thought
the person was crazy. It wouldn't have made a bit of
sense to me; why on earth would anyone be grateful for
the air they breathe?

But as my life changed from using gratitude, the things
that I took for granted or didn't give a second thought
about became an absolute miracle to me. I went from
sweating the small stuff in my little world and day-to-day
life, to opening my eyes and thinking about the bigger
picture and wonder of the Universe.

As the great scientist Newton said, "When I look at the solar system, I see the Earth at the right distance from the sun to receive the proper amounts of heat and light. This did not happen by chance."

Those words made me think more and more about the bigger picture. It's not an accident that there's a protective atmosphere surrounding us, and that beyond it there's no air or oxygen. It's not an accident that the trees give off oxygen so that our atmosphere is continually replenished. It's not an accident that our solar system is perfectly placed, and that if it were anywhere else in the galaxy we would most likely be devastated by cosmic radiation. There are thousands of parameters and ratios that support life on Earth; all of them are on a knife-edge, and their fine-tuning is so critical that a fraction of a difference in any of these parameters and ratios would make life unlivable on planet Earth. It is difficult to believe any of these things could have happened by accident. It would seem that they are perfectly designed, perfectly placed, perfectly balanced, *for* us!

When the realization hits you that all of these things might not be an accident, and that the balance of every microscopic element surrounding Earth and on Earth is in perfect harmony to support us, you will feel an overwhelming sense of gratitude for life, because all of it has been done to sustain *you!*

The magical air that you breathe is not an accident or a fluke of nature. When you think about the enormousness of what had to take place in the Universe for us to have air, and you then take a breath, breathing air into your body becomes breathtaking in every sense of the word!

We take one breath after another and never give a thought to the fact that there is always air for us to breathe. Yet oxygen is one of the most plentiful elements in our body, and as we breathe, it feeds every cell in our body so that we can continue to live. The most precious gift of our life is air, because without it, none of us would last more than a few minutes.

When I first began to use gratitude's magical power, I used it for a lot of personal things that I wanted. And it worked. But it was when I began to be grateful for the real gifts in life, that I experienced the ultimate power of gratitude. The more grateful I became for a sunset, a tree, the ocean, the dew on the grass, my life, and the people in it, every material thing I've ever dreamed of having poured down upon me. I now understand the reason why it happened that way. When we can feel truly grateful for the precious gifts of life and nature, like the magical air that we breathe, we have reached one of the deepest possible levels of gratitude. And whoever has that depth of gratitude will receive absolute abundance.

Today, stop and think about the glorious air that you breathe. Take five deliberate breaths, and feel the feeling of the air moving inside your body, and feel the joy of breathing it out. Take five full breaths in and out five different times today, and after you have taken each set of five breaths, say the magic words, "*Thank you for the magical air that I breathe,"* and be as genuinely grateful as you can for the precious, life-giving air that you breathe!

It is best if you can do this magical practice outside so you can really feel and appreciate the magnificence of fresh air, but if that's not possible then do it inside. You can close your eyes while taking the breaths, or you can do it with your eyes open. You can do it while you're walking, waiting in line, shopping, or anywhere at any time you want. The important thing is to deliberately feel the feeling of the air going in and out of your body. Breathe the way you naturally breathe, because this magical practice is not about your breathing, but about your gratitude for the air you breathe. If taking a bigger breath helps you to feel more gratitude, then do that. If it helps to make a sound or mentally say the magic words, *thank you,* as you breathe the air out, then do that. If you want you can also do a variation of this practice in the future, by imagining you're breathing in gratitude and filling yourself up with it with every breath you take.

In ancient teachings it is said that when a person reaches the point of being deeply grateful for the air that they breathe, their gratitude will have reached a new level of power, and they will have become the *true* alchemist, who can effortlessly turn every part of their life into gold!

MAGIC PRACTICE NUMBER 23

The Magical Air That You Breathe

1. Count Your Blessings: Make a list of ten blessings. Write *why* you're grateful. Reread your list, and at the end of each blessing say *thank you, thank you, thank you,* and feel as grateful for that blessing as you can.

2. **Five** times today, stop and think about the glorious air that you breathe. Take **five** deliberate breaths, and feel the feeling of the air moving inside your body, and feel the joy of breathing it out.

3. After you have taken the five breaths, say the magic words: *Thank you for the magical air that I breathe.* Be as grateful as you can for the precious, life-giving air that you breathe.

4. Just before you go to sleep tonight, hold your Magic Rock in one hand, and say the magic words, *thank you,* for the *best* thing that happened during the day.

Day 24
THE MAGIC WAND

Have you ever wished you had a magic wand so that you could just wave your wand and help the people you love? Well, today's magical practice will show you how you can use life's *real* Magic Wand to help others!

When you fervently want to help another person you have immense power, but when you direct that power with gratitude, you really do have a Magic Wand that can help the people you care about.

Energy flows where your attention goes, and so when you direct the energy of gratitude toward another person's needs, that's where the energy goes. This is the very reason why Jesus said *thank you* before he performed a miracle. Gratitude is an invisible but real force of energy, and coupled with the energy of your desire it is just like having a Magic Wand.

> *"People who wait for a magic wand fail to see that they ARE the magic wand."*
>
> THOMAS LEONARD (1955–2003)
> PERSONAL DEVELOPMENT COACH

If you have a family member, friend, or anyone you care about who is lacking physical health, in financial trouble, unhappy in their work, stressed, suffering because a relationship has ended, lost confidence in him or herself, suffering from mental problems, or feeling down about their life, you can use the invisible force of gratitude to help them with their health, wealth, and happiness.

To wave your Magic Wand for another's health, imagine that the person's health has been fully restored, and say the magic words, *thank you,* in heartfelt celebration of receiving the news that he or she is full of health again. You could imagine the person calling you to give you the news, or imagine them telling you in person, and really see and feel your reaction. When you can feel as grateful now as you would when you heard the news that the person's health had been fully restored, it will guarantee that the gratitude you feel is as sincere and as powerful as it can be.

To wave your Magic Wand to help someone you love with their wealth, follow the same magical practice, and be as grateful as if they had the wealth they needed right now. Imagine their wealth has been fully restored, it is done, and you're saying the magic words, *thank you,* because you've just received the amazing news.

If a person you know is going through a tough time, but you don't know what specifically they need, or if they need help in more than one area, then you can follow the same magical practice and wave your Magic Wand by giving thanks for their happiness, or for their health, wealth, and happiness together.

Today, choose three people you care about who are currently in need of health, wealth, or happiness, or all three. Get a photograph of each person if you have one, and keep the photographs in front of you while doing this practice.

Take the first person, hold their photograph in your hand, then close your eyes and for one minute visualize yourself receiving the news that the person has been fully restored with whatever they need. It is much easier to visualize yourself receiving the news than it is to visualize, for example, an ill person healthy again, or a depressed person happy again, or a financially stressed person abundant again. And you will feel more excitement and gratitude if you involve yourself in your visualization.

Open your eyes, and with the photograph still in your hand, say the magic words, *thank you,* slowly three times, for that person's health, wealth, or happiness, or whatever combination they need:

Thank you, thank you, thank you for
_____Name's_____ health, wealth, or happiness.

As you finish with one person, move on to the next person, and follow the same two steps until you've finished the Magic Wand practice by sending health, wealth, or happiness to all three people.

You can also use this powerful practice when you're walking down the street or going about your day and you come across someone who is obviously lacking happiness, health, or wealth. Imagine you have a Magic Wand, and in your mind wave it by giving heartfelt thanks for their wealth, health, and happiness, and know that you have set a real force of energy into motion.

Using gratitude to help someone else with his or her health, wealth, and happiness is the single greatest act of gratitude you can perform. And one of the magical things about it is that the health, wealth, and happiness you fervently wish for others, you also bring to yourself.

MAGIC PRACTICE NUMBER 24

The Magic Wand

1. Count Your Blessings: Make a list of ten blessings. Write *why* you're grateful. Reread your list, and at the end of each blessing say *thank you, thank you, thank you,* and feel as grateful for that blessing as you can.

2. Choose **three** people who you care about and who you would like to help with more health, wealth, happiness, or all three.

3. If you have them, collect a photograph of each of the three people, and keep it in front of you while doing the Magic Wand practice.

4. Take one person at a time, and hold their photograph in your hand. Close your eyes and for one minute visualize the person's health, wealth, or happiness has been fully restored, and you're receiving the news.

5. Open your eyes, and with the photograph still in your hand, say the magic words slowly: " *Thank you, thank you, thank you for ___Name's___ health, wealth, or happiness.*"

6. As you finish with one person, move on to the next person, and follow the same two steps until you've finished the Magic Wand practice for all three people.

7. Just before you go to sleep tonight, hold your
   Magic Rock in one hand, and say the magic words,
   thank you, for the *best* thing that happened during
   the day.

Day 25
CUE THE MAGIC

"Life is playfulness . . . We need to play so that we can rediscover the magic all around us."

FLORA COLAO (B. 1954)
WRITER AND THERAPIST

Today's practice, Cue The Magic, is one of my favorite practices, because it's a game you play with the Universe, and it's a lot of fun!

Imagine that the Universe is friendly and caring, and that it wants you to have everything you want in life. Because the Universe can't just walk up and hand you what you want, it uses the law of attraction to give you signs and cues to help you receive your dreams. The Universe knows you have to feel gratitude to bring forth your dreams, so it plays its part in the game by giving you personal cues to remind you to be grateful. It uses the people, circumstances, and events that surround you in your day as your magic cues to be grateful. It works like this:

If you hear an ambulance siren, the magic cue from the Universe is to be grateful for perfect health. If you see a police car, your magic cue is to be grateful for safety and security. If you see someone reading a newspaper, it's your magic cue to be thankful for great news.

If you want to change the weight of your body, when you see another person with your perfect weight, it's your magic cue from the Universe to be thankful for your perfect weight. If you want a romantic partner, when you see a couple madly in love it's your magic cue to be grateful for the perfect partner. If you want to have a family, when you see babies and children, take the magic cue and be grateful for children. When you pass by your bank, or an ATM, it's your magic cue to be grateful for plenty of money. When you arrive home, it's your magic cue to be grateful for your home, and when a neighbor calls in to have a cup of coffee, or you wave to them across the street, it's your magic cue to be grateful for your neighbors.

If you happen to see one of your material desires on your list, such as your dream house, car, motorcycle, shoes, or computer, of course it's your magic cue from the Universe to be grateful for your desire *now!*

When you begin a new day, and someone says, "Good morning," you're being given a magic cue to be grateful for the good morning. If you come across someone who is really happy, it's your magic cue to be grateful for happiness. And if you overhear another person saying *thank you,* anywhere at anytime, it's *your* magic cue to say *thank you!*

There are unlimited and creative ways the Universe has
to magically cue you to be grateful in your day-to-day
activities. You can never misunderstand a magic cue or
get a cue wrong, because whatever you think a cue is
for, you're right! The Universe uses the law of attraction
to magically cue you, and so you always attract the exact
cues that you need to be grateful for in that moment.

Cue The Magic has become a daily game I play, and
with practice, I now automatically see all the magic cues
the Universe gives me, and I give thanks for every one
of them. It never ceases to thrill and amaze me how the
Universe finds new ways to cue me to set the magic of
gratitude into motion!

When I receive a phone call from a friend or family
member, it's a cue to be grateful for him or her. When
someone says, "Isn't it a beautiful day," it's a cue to be
grateful for the beautiful weather where I live, and for
another beautiful day. If an appliance breaks down,
it's a cue to be grateful for all my appliances that are
working perfectly. If a plant in my garden is struggling,
it's a cue to be grateful for all the healthy plants in my
garden. When I collect the mail, it's a cue to be grateful
for the mail service, and for unexpected checks. When
someone says they have to go to an ATM, or I see
people in line at an ATM, it's a cue to be grateful for
money. If a person I know comes down with a sickness,
it's a cue to be grateful for their health and mine. When
I open my curtains in the morning and see the new
day, it's a cue to be grateful for the great day ahead.

And when I close my curtains at night, it's a cue to be grateful for the great day that I had.

To play Cue The Magic today, all you have to do is be alert enough to take seven magic cues from the Universe during the day, and give thanks for each one of them. For example, if you see someone with your perfect weight, say, *"Thank you for my perfect weight!"* You can never do too much gratitude, so you can choose to do more, and if you want, you can even try to respond to as many magic cues in one day as you can. If you've been following the daily magical practices over the last 24 days, you will have reached a point by now where you will be alert enough to notice the cues the Universe is always giving to you. One of the many benefits of gratitude's magical power is that it wakes you up, and makes you far more alert and aware. And the more alert and aware you become, the more grateful you become, and the more easily you attract your dreams. So, Universe – cue the magic!

MAGIC PRACTICE NUMBER 25

Cue The Magic

1. Count Your Blessings: Make a list of ten blessings.
    Write *why* you're grateful. Reread your list, and at
    the end of each blessing say *thank you, thank you,
    thank you,* and feel as grateful for that blessing as
    you can.

2. Today, be alert to what's around you, and take
    at least **seven** gratitude cues from the events in
    your day. For example, if you see someone with your
    perfect weight, say, *"Thank you for my perfect weight!"*

3. Just before you go to sleep tonight, hold your Magic
    Rock in one hand, and say the magic words, *thank
    you,* for the *best* thing that happened during the day.

Day 26

MAGICALLY TRANSFORM
MISTAKES INTO BLESSINGS

"Turn your wounds into wisdom."

OPRAH WINFREY (B. 1954)
MEDIA PERSONALITY AND BUSINESSWOMAN

Every single mistake is a blessing in disguise. Today's magical practice will prove it, because you're about to discover that there are actually untold blessings hidden within every mistake!

A child makes many mistakes while learning how to ride a bike or write, and we don't give it a second thought because we know that through their mistakes they will learn and eventually master what they're trying to do. So why is it that adults are so hard on themselves when they make a mistake? The same rule that applies to children also applies to *you*. We all make mistakes, and if we didn't make them we'd never learn anything, and we wouldn't grow any smarter or any wiser.

We have the freedom to make our own choices, and that means we have the freedom to make mistakes. Mistakes can hurt, but if we don't learn from the mistake we've made, the pain we've suffered from it has been for nothing. In fact, by the law of attraction, we will make the same mistake over and over again, until the consequences hurt us so much that we finally learn from it! It's the very reason why mistakes hurt, so that we *do* learn from them and don't make them repeatedly.

To learn from a mistake, we first have to own it, and this is where many people can become undone, because they often blame someone else for *their* mistake.

Let's consider the scenario of being pulled over by the police for speeding and being given a speeding ticket. Instead of taking responsibility for the fact that we were speeding, we blame the police because they were hiding in the bushes on the highway around a bend, we couldn't see them, they had a radar gun, and so we didn't stand a chance. But the mistake was ours, because we were the one who chose to speed.

The problem with blaming other people for our mistake is that we will still suffer the pain and consequences of our mistake, but we didn't learn from it, and so bingo! We'll attract making the same mistake again.

You are human, you will make mistakes, and it's one of the most beautiful things about being human, but you must learn from your mistakes, otherwise your life will have a lot of unnecessary pain.

How do you learn from a mistake? Gratitude!

No matter how bad something may seem, there are always, always, many things to be grateful for. When you look for as many things as you can to be grateful for in a mistake, you magically transform the mistake into blessings. Mistakes attract more mistakes, and blessings attract more blessings – which would you prefer?

Today, think about a mistake you have made in your life. It doesn't matter whether it was a big or small mistake, but choose one that still hurts when you think about it. Maybe you lost your temper with a person close to you and the relationship hasn't been the same since. Maybe you put blind faith in another person and got burned. Maybe you told a white lie to protect someone, and because of it you ended up in a difficult situation. You might have chosen the cheaper option on something, and it all went wrong and ended up costing you a whole lot more. You might have thought you were making the right decision about something, but it completely backfired on you.

Once you've chosen a mistake to magically transform into blessings, look for the things to be grateful for. To help you, there are two questions you can ask yourself:

What did I learn from the mistake?

What are the good things that came out of the mistake?

The most important things to be grateful for about every mistake are the things you learned from it. And no matter what the mistake, there are always many good things that came out of it and altered your future for the better. Think this through very carefully, and see if you can find a total of ten blessings to be grateful for. Every blessing you find has magical power. Write out your list in a gratitude journal or type them on a computer.

Let's take the example of being caught speeding by a police car and receiving a fine:

1. *I'm grateful to the police for wanting to protect me from harming myself, because after all, that was all they were trying to do.*

2. *I'm grateful to the police because if I am honest with myself, I was thinking about other things, and I wasn't concentrating on the road.*

3. *I'm grateful to the police because it was foolish to put myself at risk speeding with a tire that needed to be replaced.*

4. *I'm grateful to the police for the wake-up call. Being pulled over did affect me and it will make me watch my speed and drive more carefully in the future.*

5. *I'm grateful to the police because somehow I had a wild idea that I could speed without getting caught, and without putting myself in danger. The seriousness of the police made me face up to the fact that I was putting both myself and others in serious danger.*

6. *I'm grateful to the police because if I think about my own family being put in danger by other speeding drivers, then I definitely want the police to stop speeding drivers.*

7. *I'm really grateful to the police for the work they do in trying to ensure the safety of every person and family on the roads.*

8. *I'm grateful to the police. They must see heartbreaking situations every day, and all they're trying to do is protect my life and my family's life.*

9. *I am grateful to the police for making sure that I arrived home safely, and walked through the door to my family as I usually do.*

10. *I am grateful to the police because of all the possible consequences that could have stopped me from my speeding, the police pulling me over was the least harmful consequence, and it could have been the biggest blessing of my life.*

I would strongly urge you to take any mistakes you've made in your life that you still feel bad about, and in your own time, follow this magnificent and magical practice. Think about it; through one mistake you have the power to bring many blessings! What else guarantees dividends like that?

Magic Practice Number 26

Magically Transform Mistakes Into Blessings

1. Count Your Blessings: Make a list of ten blessings. Write *why* you're grateful. Reread your list, and at the end of each blessing say *thank you, thank you, thank you,* and feel as grateful for that blessing as you can.

2. Choose **one** mistake you made in your life.

3. Find a total of **ten** blessings you're grateful for as a result of making that mistake, and write them down.

4. To help you find blessings, you can ask yourself the questions: *What did I learn from the mistake?* And: *What are the good things that came out of the mistake?*

5. Just before you go to sleep tonight, hold your Magic Rock in one hand, and say the magic words, *thank you,* for the *best* thing that happened during the day.

Day 27

THE MAGIC MIRROR

*"The appearance of things changes according to the
emotions, and thus we see magic and beauty in them,
while the magic and beauty are really in ourselves."*

KAHLIL GIBRAN (1883–1931)
POET AND ARTIST

You can spend the rest of your life running around
trying to beat the outside world into the shape you
want, chasing one problem after another trying to fix
them, complaining about situations or other people,
and never succeed in living your life to the fullest and
realizing all of your dreams. But when you make the
magic of gratitude your way of life, everything in the
world around you magically changes – just like that.
Your world magically changes because *you* changed, so
what you are attracting changed too.

In the inspirational words of Gandhi and in the lyrics
of Michael Jackson's song, "*Man In The Mirror,*" which

impacted hundreds of millions, one of the most
powerful messages of all time was delivered:

Change the person in the mirror, and your world
will change.

If you have followed the 26 magical practices to
this point, you have changed! And even though it is
sometimes hard to see the changes in yourself, you
will have felt the change in your happiness, and you
will have seen the change of improved circumstances
in your life, and the magical changes in the world
around you.

You have practiced the magical power of gratitude for
your family and friends, for your work, money, and
health, for your dreams, and even for the people you
come across each day. But the person who deserves your
gratitude more than anyone else is you.

When you are grateful to be the person in the
mirror, feelings of dissatisfaction, discontentment,
disappointment, or I'm-not-good-enough completely
disappear. And with them, every dissatisfying,
discontenting, and disappointing circumstance in your
life magically disappears too.

Negative feelings about yourself cause the greatest
damage to your life, because they are more powerful
than any feelings you have about anything or anyone
else. Wherever you go and whatever you do you take
those negative feelings with you in every moment,
and those feelings taint everything you touch, and

they act as a magnet, attracting more dissatisfaction, discontentment, and disappointment with everything you do.

When you are grateful to be *you,* you will only attract circumstances that make you feel even better about yourself. You have to be rich with good feelings about yourself to bring the riches of life to you. Gratitude for yourself enriches you!

*"Whoever has **gratitude** (for themselves) will be given more, and he or she will have an abundance. Whoever does not have **gratitude** (for themselves), even what he or she has will be taken from him or her."*

To do the Magic Mirror practice, go to a mirror right now. Look directly at the person in the mirror, and out loud say the magic words, *thank you,* with all your heart. Mean it more than you ever have before. Say *thank you* for being you! Say *thank you* for everything that you are! Say *thank you* with at least the same amount of feeling you've used for everything and everyone else! Be grateful for *you* just as you are!

Continue with the Magic Mirror practice by being grateful to that beautiful person in the mirror for the rest of the day today, and say the magic words, *thank you,* every time you look at yourself in a mirror. If you're not in a position to say the magic words out loud at any particular time, then you can say them in your mind. And if you're *really* brave, you can look in the Magic Mirror and say three things about yourself that you're grateful for.

If for any reason in the future you are not being kind to yourself, you will know to give to the one person who deserves your gratitude more than anyone else – the person in the mirror!

When you're grateful, you don't blame yourself when you make a mistake. When you're grateful, you don't criticize yourself when you're not perfect. When you're grateful for being you, you are happy, and you will become a magnet to happy people, happy situations, and magical circumstances, which will surround you wherever you go and in whatever you do. When you can see the magic in that person in the mirror, your whole world will change!

Magic Practice Number 27

The Magic Mirror

1. Count Your Blessings: Make a list of ten blessings.
    Write *why* you're grateful. Reread your list, and at
    the end of each blessing say *thank you, thank you,
    thank you,* and feel as grateful for that blessing as
    you can.

2. Each time you look at yourself in a mirror today,
    say *thank you,* and mean it more than you ever
    have before.

3. If you're really brave, while looking in the mirror
    say **three** things you're grateful for about yourself.

4. Just before you go to sleep tonight, hold your Magic
    Rock in one hand, and say the magic words, *thank
    you,* for the *best* thing that happened during the day.

Day 28
REMEMBER THE MAGIC

> *"That's the thing with magic. You've got to know it's still here, all around us, or it just stays invisible for you."*

CHARLES DE LINT (B. 1951)
WRITER AND CELTIC FOLK MUSICIAN

Every day is unique; there is no day like any other day. The good things that happen each day are forever different and forever changing, and so when you Remember The Magic by counting yesterday's blessings, no matter how many times you do it, it will be different every time. It's just one of the reasons why Remember The Magic is the most powerful ongoing practice to maintain the magic of gratitude in your life. No matter what your desires are now, or what desires you will have in the future, this magical practice will remain the most powerful practice for your entire life.

The easiest way to remember the blessings of yesterday is to start by remembering the beginning of the day when you woke up, and go back over the day in your mind, recollecting the major events of the morning, afternoon, and evening, until you reach the time when you went to bed. When you recall yesterday's blessings it should be effortless; you are just scanning the surface of yesterday, and as you scan, the blessings will bubble to the surface of your mind.

You can start this magical practice by asking the question:

What are the good things that happened yesterday?

Whenever you ask a question, your mind will immediately look for the answer. Did you receive any great news? Did you magically receive or accomplish one of your desires? Did you magically receive unexpected money? Did you feel especially happy? Did you hear from a friend who you haven't heard from in a long time? Did something go magnificently well for you? Did you receive a great phone call or email? Did you receive a compliment, or did someone express his or her appreciation for you? Did someone help you to solve a problem? Did you help somebody? Did you finish a project or start something new you're excited about? Did you eat your favorite food, or watch a great movie? Did you receive a gift, resolve a situation, have a stimulating meeting, quality time with someone, a great conversation, or make plans for something you really want to do?

Remember The Magic and list yesterday's blessings on a computer, or write them out in a journal. Scan over the surface of yesterday until you feel satisfied that you've recalled the blessings of the day. They can be small things or big things, because it's not about the size of the blessings; it's about how many blessings you find, and how much gratitude you feel for each one. As you remember and notate each one, simply be grateful and say the magic words for it – *thank you.*

When you want to do this magical practice after today, you can mix it up, so that some days you write out the blessings and other days you remember the blessings and say them out loud or in your mind. You can make a quick list of the blessings, or you can make a more detailed list saying why you're grateful for each one.

There is no set number of blessings to find from yesterday, because every day is different. But I can assure you that every single day of your life is full of blessings, and when you have opened your eyes to see the truth of this, you will have opened your heart to the magic of life, and your life will be abundant and magnificent.

"Whoever has **gratitude** *will be given more, and he or she will have an abundance. Whoever does not have* **gratitude**, *even what he or she has will be taken from him or her."*

Remember The Magic – it was created for *you!*

Magic Practice Number 28

Remember The Magic

1. Count Your Blessings: Make a list of ten blessings. Write *why* you're grateful. Reread your list, and at the end of each blessing say *thank you, thank you, thank you,* and feel as grateful for that blessing as you can. You have written 280 blessings over the course of this book!

2. Remember The Magic by counting the blessings of yesterday, and writing them down. Ask yourself the question: *What are the good things that happened yesterday?* Scan the surface of yesterday until you feel satisfied that you've remembered and written down all the blessings of the day.

3. As you remember each one, simply say the magic words, *thank you,* for it in your mind.

4. After today you can do this practice as a written list, or out loud or in your mind. You can make a quick list of the things you're grateful for about yesterday, or make a shorter and more detailed list and say why you're grateful for them.

5. Just before you go to sleep tonight, hold your Magic Rock in one hand, and say the magic words, *thank you,* for the *best* thing that happened during the day.

Your Magical Future

You are the builder of your life, and gratitude is your magical tool to build the most incredible life. You have now laid a foundation through these magical practices, and with the tool of gratitude, you are adding more floors to the building of your life. Your life will climb higher and higher, until you touch the stars. There is no end to the heights you can reach with gratitude, and there's no end to the magic you can experience. Like the stars in the Universe, it's infinite!

> *"To speak gratitude is courteous and pleasant, to enact gratitude is generous and noble, but to live gratitude is to touch Heaven."*
>
> JOHANNES A. GAERTNER (1912–1996)
> PROFESSOR, THEOLOGIAN, POET

The ideal way to move forward from here is to maintain the foundation of gratitude you've built, and gradually keep building on it through increasing your depth of feeling. The more you practice gratitude, the deeper you will be able to feel it, and the more deeply you feel it, the less time you will need to give to it. As a guide:

Three days a week of Remember The Magic, or combining it with two other magical practices of your choosing, should maintain your current foundation of gratitude, and keep building the magic in your life so that your life continues to get better and better. For example, you might choose to do Remember The Magic on one day, Magical Relationships on the second, and Magic Money on the third day.

Four days a week of Remember The Magic, or incorporating it with three other magical practices of your choosing, will maintain your gratitude *and* accelerate the magic.

Five days a week of Remember The Magic, or incorporating it with four other magical practices of your choosing, will dramatically increase your happiness and the magic in every area and circumstance of your life.

Six or seven days a week of Remember The Magic, or incorporating it with any other magical practices of your choosing, and you will become the true alchemist, who can turn everything into gold!

Magic Practice Recommendations

To keep the magic continuing in the important areas of your life, like your happiness, health, relationships, career, money, and the material things you own, you could do the specific practices for each area once a week. However, if you want to *increase* the magic in any area of your life, you should give more through an increased practice of gratitude for that area, several days a week. If you are unwell, you will want to do the magical practices for your health every day, if not multiple times in a day.

The following recommendations will easily guide you toward the magical practices that will have the strongest and fastest effect in that area. Follow the recommendations in the relevant area for three weeks minimum, doing each recommended practice once a week:

RELATIONSHIPS

Magical Relationships   *page 18*

Magic Dust Everyone – *page 109*

Magically Heal Your Relationships – *page 147*

The Magic Wand – *page 211*
(The Magic Wand practice can be used on people you know using photographs, or on people you don't know without photographs.)

The Magic Mirror – *page 233*

Remember The Magic – *page 238*

HEALTH

Magical Health – *page 58*

Magic Dust Everyone – *page 109*

Magic And Miracles In Health – *page 155*

The Magical Air That You Breathe – *page 205*

The Magic Wand – *page 211*
*(The Magic Wand practice can be used on people you
know using photographs, or on people you don't know
without photographs.)*

Remember The Magic – *page 238*

MONEY

Magic Money – *page 66*

The Money Magnet – *page 99*
*(If you haven't done the Money Magnet magical practice
before, make sure you complete all steps at least once. If you're
repeating this practice, you can jump to step 4.)*

The Magic Check – *page 163*

The Magic Wand – *page 211*
*(The Magic Wand practice can be used on people you
know using photographs, or on people you don't know
without photographs.)*

The Magic Mirror – *page 233*

Remember The Magic – *page 238*

CAREER

Works Like Magic – *page 74*

Magic Dust Everyone – *page 109*

The Magic Wand – *page 211*
(When using The Magic Wand practice for your career, you can also send success to people. Wishing success for others will accelerate the success in your own life.

The Magic Wand practice can be used on people you know using photographs, or on people you don't know without photographs.)

The Magic Mirror – *page 233*

Remember The Magic – *page 238*

YOUR DESIRES

Magic Dust Everyone – *page 109*

Make All Your Wishes Come True – *page 129*
(If you haven't done the practice of Make All Your Wishes Come True before, make sure you complete all the steps at least once. If you're repeating this practice, you can jump to step 3.)

Before Your Very Eyes – *page 199*

The Magic Wand – *page 211*
(*The Magic Wand practice can be used on people you know using photographs, or on people you don't know without photographs.*)

The Magic Mirror – *page 233*

Remember The Magic – *page 238*

Your Magic Rock

You can make The Magic Rock practice a part of your daily life, by continuing to keep your Magic Rock by your bedside, and using the time you get into bed as your reminder to be grateful for the best thing that happened that day. You can also carry your Magic Rock with you in your pocket, and every time you touch it, use it as your reminder to think of something you're grateful for.

Your Magic Dust

You can also make The Magic Dust Everyone practice a part of your daily life. Other than sprinkling magic dust over the people who serve you, there are many more ways to continue using this practice. You can sprinkle magic dust over everyone and everything! If your boss is a bit grumpy, you can secretly sprinkle magic dust over him or her. You can sprinkle magic dust over a family member or loved one if they're in a bad mood, or anyone you come across who needs some magic in their life. You can also add magic wherever you go, and sprinkle magic dust over babies and children, over your plants or garden, your food and drinks, your computer or your mail before you open them, your wallet, car, your phone before you take or make a phone call, or over any circumstance that you want to improve. The many applications of magic dust are limited only by your imagination!

THE MAGIC NEVER ENDS

I practice gratitude every day of my life, and it's inconceivable to me now that I could have lived days, months, and years without practicing gratitude in some way every day. Gratitude has become a part of my personality, it is in my cells, and it's a pattern in my subconscious mind.

But if we get caught up in life and forget to practice gratitude, over a period of time, the magic will evaporate. I use the magic in my life as my guide to let me know if I'm practicing gratitude enough, or if I need to practice more. I watch my life carefully, and if I find that I'm not feeling as happy, I increase my practice of gratitude. If a few little problems start appearing in a particular area of my life, immediately I increase the magical practices of gratitude in that area.

I'm not blinded by false appearances anymore. Instead I look for the goodness to be grateful for in every circumstance, *knowing* that it's there. And then, like a puff of smoke, what was unwanted magically disappears!

"I started out giving thanks for small things, and the more thankful I became, the more my bounty increased. That's because what you focus on expands, and when you focus on the goodness in your life, you create more of it. Opportunities, relationships, even money flowed my way when I learned to be grateful no matter what happened in my life."

OPRAH WINFREY (B. 1954)
MEDIA PERSONALITY AND BUSINESSWOMAN

Through the practice of gratitude you are using an infallible law of the Universe; it is a gift from the Universe to you, and it exists in order for you to *use it* and advance your life.

The Universe and You

There is a level that you can reach with gratitude that causes *unlimited* abundance in your life. The way that this level of gratitude is reached is through your relationship with the Universe, or, if you prefer, Spirit or God.

You can tend to think of the Universe as separate from you, and when you think of it, look up above yourself and toward the sky. While the Universe most certainly is above you, it is also below you, and behind you, and beside you, and it is within every single thing and every single person. That means the Universe is *within you*.

"As below, so above; and as above so below. With this knowledge alone you may work miracles."

THE EMERALD TABLET (CIRCA 5,000–3,000 BC)

When you understand that the Universe is *within* you, and by it's very nature it is *for* you, wanting you to have *more* life, *more* health, *more* love, *more* beauty, and *more* of everything you want, then you will feel genuine gratitude to the Universe for *everything* you receive in your life. And you will have established a personal relationship between you and the Universe.

The more genuine gratitude you feel toward the Universe for everything you receive, the closer your relationship becomes with the Universe – and that is when you can reach the level of *unlimited* abundance from the magic of gratitude.

You will have opened your heart and mind completely to the magic of gratitude, and with it you will touch the lives of everyone you come into contact with. You will become a friend of the Universe. You will become a channel for unlimited blessings on Earth. When you get up close and personal with the Universe, when you feel that closeness of the Universe within you, from that moment on, the world will belong to you, and there will be nothing that you cannot be, have, or do!

Gratitude Is the Answer

Gratitude is the cure for broken or difficult relationships, for lack of health or money, and for unhappiness. Gratitude eliminates fear, worry, grief, and depression, and brings happiness, clarity, patience, kindness, compassion, understanding, and peace of mind. Gratitude brings solutions to problems, and the opportunities and wherewithal to realize your dreams.

Gratitude is behind every success, and it opens the door to new ideas and discoveries, as the great scientists Newton and Einstein proved. Imagine if every scientist followed in their footsteps; the world would be propelled into new territories of understanding, growth, and advancement. Current limits would be broken, and life-altering discoveries would be made in technology, physics, medicine, psychology, astronomy, and every scientific field.

If gratitude became a mandatory subject in schools, we would see a generation of children who would advance our civilization through spectacular accomplishments and discoveries, obliterating disagreements, ending wars, and bringing peace to the world.

The nations who will lead the world in the future are the ones whose leaders and people are the most grateful. The gratitude of a nation's people would cause their country to thrive and become rich, would cause illnesses and disease to drastically drop, businesses and production to escalate, and happiness and peace to sweep the nation. Poverty would disappear, and there would not be a single person in hunger, because a grateful nation could never allow it to exist.

The more people who discover gratitude's magical power, the faster it will sweep the world, and cause a gratitude revolution.

Take The Magic with You

Take gratitude with you wherever you go. Saturate the magic of gratitude into your passions, encounters, actions, and life situations to make all your dreams come true. In the future, if life presents you with a challenging situation that you think you have no control over, and you're at a loss as to what to do, instead of worry or fear, turn to the magic of gratitude and be grateful for *everything else* in your life. When you deliberately thank the goodness in your life, the circumstances around the challenging situation will magically change.

> *"We showed him (i.e. man) the way: whether he be grateful or ungrateful (rests on his will)."*
>
> KORAN (AL-INSÂN 76:3)

Say the magic words, *thank you.* Say them out loud, shout them from the rooftops, whisper them to yourself, say them in your mind, or feel them in your heart, but wherever you go from this day forward, take gratitude and its magical power with you.

To have a magical life filled with abundance and happiness, the answer is on your lips, it is inside your heart, and it is ready and waiting for you to bring forth *the magic!*

Rhonda Byrne

About Rhonda Byrne

Rhonda began her journey with *The Secret* film, viewed by millions across the planet. She followed with *The Secret* book, a global bestseller, available in 47 languages and with over 20 million copies in print.

The Secret has remained on the *New York Times* bestseller list for 190 weeks, and was recently named by *USA Today* as one of the top 20 bestselling books of the past 15 years.

Rhonda continued her groundbreaking work with *The Power* in 2010, also a *New York Times* bestseller, and now available in 43 languages.